INSTITUTE FOR EASTWEST STUDIES
NEW YORK · PRAGUE · BUDAPEST

THE UNCERTAIN STATE OF THE RUSSIAN ECONOMY

**Published in
cooperation
with the
Institute of
Economic Policy
(Moscow)**

Distributed by Westview Press
        5500 Central Avenue
        Boulder, Colorado 80301

CIP Data is available

TABLE OF CONTENTS

Table of Contents--Continued

Introduction

Kálmán Mizsei

It could not be more topical than now, on the eve of the Congress of Peoples' Deputies meeting in Moscow, to publish the economic analysis of the Institute of Economic Policy (IEP). The Moscow-based think-tank was established by Acting Prime Minister Yegor Gaidar and is generally considered his government's domestic intellectual "backyard." The private research institute hosts most of the progressive Russian economists at the forefront of the nation's economic reform movement.

While it is timely to publish the analysis of IEP regardless of the outcome of the major political fight of the year, it is very tricky to write an introduction to it just before the Congress opens. The perspectives of the country will vary enormously depending on the outcome of the political battle. The paper is published at a critical moment for Russian society. A large-scale straightforward experiment with building a capitalist economy started after the failure of the August 1991 coup and the subsequent demise of Mikhail Gorbachev. Although in East Central Europe we had a long track record with economic reform, the Russian situation differed in many respects from the outset. The scale of the country, its historical authoritarian structures, and its more recent institutional setup and rigid economy (prices, plan directives, closed economy and also society) are the most important dimensions to list.

The reforms have mobilized antagonistic forces in society. The old-line communist ideologues and apparatchiks are desperate because they are losing power; the top managers of the so-called military-industrial complex (MIC) are horrified with the prospect of further decreasing military expenditure and subsidies; nationalists are finding it hard to digest losing control over frontier territories of the ex-Soviet empire and the emergence of national movements inside the Russian Republic itself.

At the moment, the best possible compromise in the field of economy seems to be that between the radical reformers and industrialists. However, the problem is that the other great dilemma of the Russian society, namely the trauma of suddenly losing control over large parts of the ex-imperium, divides the political forces at different lines than the economic question. This is especially problematic for the Civic Union led by Arkady Volsky; part of the group would opt for pragmatic solutions, for acknowledging the existing realities. A large faction of the Union, however, cannot conntenance the constant experience of "national shame" and on this basis is willing to cooperate more with the "brown-red coalition" than with the Gaidar team. For them, the very existence of the Gaidar government is a continuous outrage.

Besides its obvious political nastiness, the problem with the strength of the "imperialist" approach to the economy is that if it gains some control over the government, it will cause a major setback for the cause of economic reform. The nationalist coalition is, namely, much more collectivist in its economic approach than even the more pragmatic segments of the Volsky group. Time is extremely critical in the current game. At the moment, the radical reformist, "Westernizer" team is very thin. Almost as in the case of Stolypin reforms at the beginning of the century, its fate seems to depend almost entirely on the "czar," this time on Yeltsin. This is so in spite the fact that the societal differences between the Russian society of the two periods are, of course, immense. The recent one is basically a highly educated complex urban society (although with a large backward rural population), presumably much more receptive to ideas of a free economy and society than the one nearly 90 years ago. However, to establish a firmer constituency for the free market needs some time. What is happening now is a race with time for the Gaidar team.

It applies especially to the government's privatization-strategy. It was the impression of the radical reformers for quite a few years that privatization was feasible in the given political structures only if top managers of the state enterprises had an incentive to support denationalization of their own firms. In the recent Russian legislative framework, this "insiderist" strategy was skillfully merged into a general "mass privatization" concept. Recent near-hyperinflation has made access to enterprise assets extremely cheap through voucher-options offered to employees and managers. Therefore, what has been politically unfeasible in other reforming countries, i.e., selling assets cheap to insiders, has suddenly become technically possible in the Russia situation. This is another aspect of the race with time, in at least two respects.

On one hand, the insiderist strategy will soon invite protests as cheap buy-offs, as well as concentration of vouchers in the hands of few investors, recently shopping around the whole country, becomes more and more public.

On the other hand, perhaps most importantly, the radical reformers expect that the privatization will change the nature of the political battle. Political coalitions are not static,

3

but rather are dynamic phenomena. It is particularly true in a situation of dramatic changes in society and the economy. As the IEP analysis demonstrates, the "Gaidar boys" hope, and in fact desperately need, that the coalition of enterprise bosses, skillfully kept together by Volsky, will rapidly fragment as privatization moves ahead. The more rapid the privatization of large enterprises, the more difficult it will be for the politicians to keep the coalition together. (It is similar with exporters: as soon as there are no particular administrative barriers to exports, producers for foreign markets will largely support opening and free prices. That is why it has probably been a mistake not to eliminate traditional barriers to exports more than actually happened.) Heavy attack from the conservatives in this respect is rational: a year from now it will be a different Russia, and any conservative restoration will probably have a much narrower social base than now. The current privatization policy is an appropriate approach by Anatoly Chubais, deputy prime minister responsible for privatization, to the matter.

Runaway inflation makes the recent privatization strategy technically more feasible. However, it imposes another danger on the general perspectives of economic reform. My impression is that in the last few months the Russian reformers have tacitly decided that, because of apparently insurmountable political and institutional obstacles, they must accept for a while the reality of moving towards hyperinflation while they concentrate on radicalization of the structural reforms. The strategy is understandable also because it seems to be very difficult to impose payment discipline on firms if the business culture in the country does not change dramatically mainly through reform of property rights and of contract enforcement. The lack of such discipline threatens that finances will go out of state control.

The trouble with this strategy is that if the agents of the economy get accustomed to the recent level of price dynamism (not to mention hyperinflation), as is the case with Latin American countries, it will be utterly difficult to get away with. Uncertainty created by current macroeconomic imbalances will make potential private investors extremely cautious. In this respect it is of secondary importance whether they invest by way of privatization or by opening new businesses.

Why is it so much more difficult to achieve macroeconomic stability in Russia than in many other reform economies? The general answer is obvious: given history, tradition, inherited institutional and political conditions and the mentality of society, Russia started with much worse conditions than the "fast-track" reformers of the region, i.e., Czechoslovakia, Hungary and Poland. However, the story of the Balcerowicz program teaches us that carefully selected programs and determination in implementation can make some difference. Comparison with the Polish stabilization measures at the beginning of 1990 can highlight some interesting points. In Poland, stabilization was also accompanied by bold liberalization of the price system and, actually much more than in Russia, of foreign trade. However, the political setting, as well as some important elements of the programs were very different. Both Balcerowicz and Gaidar enjoyed at the beginning the support of their political mentors (the Solidarity leadership in Poland and Yeltsin in Russia). The Polish situation was more difficult from the side of organized labor. Both the traditional labor unions and Solidarity tried to soften the rigor of the program. In Russia there were no "real" nationwide unions in the beginning of the program and the existing ones proved to be quite cooperative, out of understandable self-interest. The question then emerges whether liberalization of the wage system was really necessary in Russia.

In Russia, however, the powerful "military-industrial complex" (MIC) has been a major obstacle to reform; this kind of force, appealing to many as a relic of the Soviet Union's international significance, was not there in Poland.[1] However, one is tempted to believe that the major short-run problem of the recent Russian reforms is not even the MIC itself but, paradoxically, the independence of a central bank which cooperates more with the industrial lobby than with the reformist government. Credit expansion in the Russian economy became independent of government action and this way has practically jeopardized the stabilization efforts. The problem has been aggravated by the disintegration of the ruble zone; in particular, the other newly independent countries were able to generate ruble credit for quite a long period of time.

Understandably, economic relations with the rest of the CIS is a major dilemma for the new Russian establishment, which is reflected in this document. Economic rationality itself would have called long ago for cutting monetary ties with those new nations which do not want to surrender credit creation to the Central Bank of Russia; in the field of trade, world market prices should result in tremendous gains in terms of trade for Russia, just as it has

---

[1] It is worth mentioning that MIC includes a very large part of non-military production. So, for instance, military enterprises produce the entire domestic production of television sets, sewing machines, cameras, VCRs. Overwhelming is their share in the production of refrigerators, stereo equipment, vacuum cleaners, computers and many other goods of industrial use. (See *Economic Newsletter,* Russian Research Center, Harvard University, Vol. XVI., No.3. November 15, 1992.)

with COMECON members. Political considerations make the Russian decision-makers very cautious; they seem to believe that such a move would further "disintegrate" the ex-Soviet Union. Even more dubious is the fear of some that this would cause economic harm for Russia as well. In fact, as the last two years of COMECON also show, reorientation of trade can happen much more rapidly than is generally perceived.

While the program started in a high but, unlike in Poland, not-yet-hyperinflationary environment, in the period of the publication of this document, the dynamics of the consumer price index have reached 30% per month. Besides the monetary policy, the fiscal arena also needs a sustained effort; as the analysis of the "Gaidar institute" says, the deficit in certain months reached almost 15%; because of the lack of capital markets and a poor savings culture, virtually the whole amount had to be monetized. In recent months, one might have observed a marked improvement in the deficit; however, the Polish story also tells us that a sustained balance in the public finances is what really counts in the long run.

This is, therefore, a different psychological situation than in Poland. The Balcerowicz team could always get legitimacy from the fact that it successfully killed the inflationary spiral; the recent Russian economic policy, many can seemingly claim, has "led" the economy into one. From this perspective, it is much more difficult for the government to start with a new stabilization program now. However, it is badly needed. Moreover, there are few economists in Russia other than Gaidar's team who would yet have the intellectual capacity of realizing it without a major retreat from the liberalization course. Compared with notoriously inflationary economies, Russia has the precious benefit that neither the economy nor the households are yet accustomed to large inflation. Therefore indexation mechanisms, constituting in other cases a major obstacle, are not widespread. However, this is only a question of time, as quarterly indexation in the case of minimum wages has already been introduced.

However, the lack of payment discipline in the economy is widespread. In the last two years, the central bank has "trained" the state enterprises that, however dark their liquidity situation, they will be bailed out with cheap credit. (Interest rates are sharply negative in real terms.) This logic has to be broken with a credible policy. Balcerowicz had one, but the forced interenterprise credits and the lack of credible bankruptcy deterrent still caused a major headache. It will be even more difficult in the business culture of Russia, with the banking system as it is, to turn around expectations of the economic agents. However, no one can save this operation for the Russian government.

The careful reader of the analysis will discover a seemingly contradictory situation in the text. The authors argue that in Russia, in spite of the rapidly growing inflation, household incomes expanding more rapidly than expenses, and sharply negative real rates of interest, there is seemingly no flight from money, which would be reflected in skyrocketing velocity of money. There is a tremendous statistical problem the monetary analysis has to face. However, there are some other, unconventional reasons to offer at least partial explanation for the contradiction.[2] Velocity of the money is determined by technical factors as well as by supply and demand. It appears that in the period of analysis, the government introduced an innovation of regional clearing houses, which actually turned out to slow down money transfer instead of accelerating it. Secondly, in the period of April-June 1992, the country

---

[2] This considerations I largely owe to the consultations with Alexander Tsapin.

8

witnessed a severe cash crisis. The income that appears in household statistics might be seriously overestimated. Any households receiving their incomes a few months later suffered a large depreciation in real terms (no indexation was applied). Therefore the income statistics published in the text may be misleading. Thirdly, there may be another factor: prices of durable goods have grown generally faster than those for everyday use. Probably, the lower income strata (a very large proportion of the Russian society) has been able to maintain its consumption of basic goods but had to reduce its purchase of durables, even in case of increased money hoarding. Outside the big cities, it is still difficult to find alternative portfolio, e.g., hard currencies. One also believes that in 1992 a larger part of retail turnover has remained unregistered than earlier, as legal and illegal private businesses mushroom. Actually, the data of the Savings Bank of the Russian Federation do show a dramatic deterioration in the populations savings in real terms as well as in comparison to salaries.[3]

One can appreciate the real difficulties of analyzing the Russian economy only by taking into account the state of macroeconomic and monetary statistics. It should also be underlined that the paper was written in September; it is especially apparent in the still-too-optimistic look at the monetary policy of the country.

The analysis of the young staff of IEP presented in this publication is a remarkable effort at understanding the nature of the macroeconomic trouble. I have been particularly impressed with Alexander Tsapin, whose collaboration on this volume was critical. Without

---

[3] According to data provided by Pavel I. Zhikharev, Chairman of the Savings Bank

Dr. Tsapin, IEWS Director of Publications Richard Levitt, and Word Processing Officer Amy Lew, this publication could not have been prepared in such record time.

The bitter truth is that at present, Russia badly needs a new stabilization shock. Oil and gas prices are 10 to 20 times lower than world market prices. Yet inflation is already dangerously high. It will, unfortunately, be as painful an adjustment as the one at the beginning of 1992. However, the choice is between this and a retreat to central control of prices and businesses. If the Congress leaves room for Yeltsin to move ahead, in the next few months the operation must start. More delay will mean widespread indexation, the emergence of more fierce organized labor and other lobbies which will make the perspectives of stabilization all the more bleak.

New York, December 2, 1992.

Executive Summary

Alexander Tsapin

By the summer of 1992, the underlying trends of Russia's political and economic development were clear, making it possible to figure out both the directions economic indicators were moving in and which motives were driving the major political forces in society. But such "clarity" was only relative, because future trends, always difficult to predict, are that much more uncertain because of the inadequate reaction of Russian economic agents to changing regimes.

The explicit stratification of the Russian political establishment was one of the most important results of the socioeconomic processes of the first half of the year. The reformist bloc presented by Boris Yeltsin and the young government team led by Acting Prime Minister Yegor Gaidar pursued policies basically consistent with a program of stabilization. The centrist bloc under by Civic Union leader Arkady Volsky was the major opposition force, representing the interests of industrial and agrarian lobbies and demanding a more gradual transition to a free market system. The hard-line bloc represented by the ironic union of former communists (e.g., Sergei Baburin) and chauvinists (the National Salvation Front) gained some strength, using the instability and frustration in society due to painful adjustment. It became clear, however, that neither pure radical reformist approach, nor restoration of an administratively-run economic system were viable development strategies. Political compromise seemed to be required, especially if progress was to be made in the

11

four key thrusts of economic policy emerging in the first half of the year: price liberalization, financial stabilization, privatization and liberalization of foreign economic relations.

Although accompanied by a substantial decrease in output, liberalization of prices led to elimination of large discrepancies between demand and supply, improvement of price proportions and creation of incentives for more rational economic behavior. As a result of tight monetary policy and financial restrictions in the first quarter of the year, inflation dropped from 350% in January to 7% in July. At the same time, the reaction of state-owned enterprises was quite different from that which could be expected. Instead of cutting costs (including labor) and searching for new market opportunities, the producers replied by curtailing mutual payments and exerting strong pressure on establishment institutions--both government and parliament--to loosen credit and other financial restrictions.

In the second quarter, the government and the central bank were forced to increase credit to finance agricultural activity and the supply of goods to northern regions of the country; measures on settling the payments crisis were taken (partial cancellation of enterprises' mutual arrears). The budget deficit, which seemed to be at sustainable levels in the first quarter (3.8% of GNP), substantially deteriorated in the second quarter (approximately 13% of GNP in the first seven months) due to the first wave of indexation of salaries in public sector and continuing subsidies. As a result, future inflation pressure was building.

Privatization was relatively the most successful element of the reform policy. A large network of privatization agencies was created, covering the whole territory of the country, and many normative documents were adopted, laying the foundation for triggering the privatization process. The first results of auctions and tenders showed the opportunities for dynamic transformation of the property rights sytem. While not without serious shortcomings, the government policy seems to have achieved an important result--the idea that mass privatization and incentive creation for top managers and employees of state-owned enterprises are compatible.

The liberalization of foreign economic relations cannot be characterized unambiguously. Reduction of import tariffs, development of a foreign exchange market, and the creation of free economic zones have been accompanied by adoption of contradictory legislation and insufficiently articulated rules for foreign capital participation in the privatization process. Russia's current account is in deficit due to increasing debt servicing payments, and one can also observe a decline in direct foreign investment. This reflects the low level of the foreign investors' confidence under the conditions of political and economic instability. At the same time, Russia has tremendous investment potential, owing to rich natural resource deposits, a rather skilled and inexpensive labor force, and sophisticated technologies in the sectors of the economy to be converted.

1. Social-Political Processes

V.A. Mau
I.P. Vassilyeva
V.V. Stupin

A. *The Social-Political Situation in Society*

The radical transformation of the socio-economic system dominating in Russia for decades began in a complicated situation. In late 1991, there was no solid hope for genuine improvement in economic policy, and the widespread pessimism was confirmed by the results of sociological investigation and opinion polls. Yet, with real socio-economic transformation on the horizon, there appeared a chance to reject the standard logic of revolutionary crisis (when the polarization of forces is followed by a social explosion and the establishment of dictatorship) and carry out radical reform through politically "soft" and peaceful methods.

Though there was no explosion at the end of 1991, the population was exhausted and inclined to turn down slogans and ideas calling for violence, war and class confrontation. Boris Yeltsin was himself quite popular, although he headed a government of unpopular reforms; there were no indications of a "revolution of expectations," the hopes for an "economic miracle" disappeared, and practically two-thirds of the population did not believe that there would be an opportunity to overcome the crisis without lowering living standards.

Since the end of 1991, the economic slump has gradually come to be viewed as unmanageable. The government's actions aimed at liberalizing the economy showed the real

14

depth of the crisis and made the drop in living standards much clearer than it was before. All this drew people's attention to the economic aspects of the politicians' activities. The situation in the national economy came to be a meaningful factor in carrying out political processes. In other words, it is economics that in the foreseeable future will become the decisive battlefield of the political struggle.

Some social and political improvement can be seen now, nearly a year into reform:

- The refusal of a considerable part of the population to continue pattern stereotypes and aspirations is evident. The reliance of the Russian people on their own forces for survival under crisis conditions is becoming the leading principle in their conduct. Rigid demands to the government put forward by the participants of the meetings and strikes no longer reflect, as a rule, a clearly dependent character.

- Enterprises are becoming truly independent actors of the economic process. State enterprises have, in the main, overcome the rigid branch system of administration and show no wish to join any structure similar to a branch ministry.

- Now one speaks mainly about the danger of the disintegration of Russia, similar to that of the USSR. If, in late 1991, regional administrations in various ways prevented a single all-Russia market from functioning, at present the situation has considerably changed. The liberalization of prices and balanced demand limitations make administrative bans senseless (with the exception of some national republics in federation of Russia, but here one is faced with overarching concrete national and political problems).

B. *The Position of the Government*

By the spring of 1992, the new position of the reform, its successes and, particularly, its failures had assumed clear shape.

By May, it was obvious that hopes for rapid macroeconomic stability had not been fulfilled. The problem of financial stability cannot be solved without touching upon the problem of "structural perestroika." Also, most conservative industrial and agricultural circles quickly recovered from the demoralization caused by the failure of the attempted coup in August.

The MIC (Military Industrial Complex) and the agricultural lobby in the parliament and outside started an active struggle for increasing their share of the state budget. If in the beginning, when stabilizing activities began to be applied, the government found it easy to restrain the wishes of branch groupings, by the end of spring the burden of unpopular decisions and compromise which the government had to make began to limit the possibilities for carrying out the originally planned course. The President and the government had to choose between further unpopular measures or a gradual smothering of the current policy.

To radicalize the chosen reform course required limitations essentially on the rights of the parliament (Supreme Soviet) and a reliance on only the President's power to implement the reforms. It could, in turn, mean an open fight with the enterprise directors corps, which had actively obstructed the reform. This option could lead to mass bankruptcy and increased--possibly unwelcome--access to the national economy for foreign producers. In the long run, such overt opposition is unacceptable, because a powerful consolidated opposition of previously isolated political forces might have come into being.

In such a situation, to keep the strategic reform course unchanged, the government has to go over from the tough and extremely time-compressed measures of macroeconomic stabilization to the policy of a "position" type, meaning rather long and complicated maneuvers in both social and economic spheres.

A coalition government becomes a reality as the necessity arises to form a sufficient social basis for the given course. Such a coalition would rely on the enterprise directors of

16

the state-owned enterprises which are moving toward market conditions, for with them there appears a possibility for cooperation with business structures.

Yet, the very formation of such a coalition casts doubt on the political stability of the reformist team and its ability to realize or control the reform progress. One can say that the government was forced to become an independent *political* force, to renounce its image of reform technologists. In its turn, that will make it possible for the team to widen the fields for maneuvers at the expense of attracting prominent representatives of the enterprise directors, to form more open procedures for the elaboration of mutually acceptable decisions, to replace the "backstage" lobby and to legalize it.

The reformists will be able to blame inflation on the performance of their partners from the government coalition, a political safety valve. For industrialists, it will be possible to create conditions the hindering fast collapse of production because of the tough monetary policy.

The main thing will be to keep inflation at a socially acceptable level while finding a way to identify effective keys for the control of credit policy. Meanwhile, the actual passing of big enterprises into the hands of enterprise directors with varied interests may make it possible to split the managerial lobby, which will strengthen the executive power in the cause of reform.

However, external economic conditions may be problematic. Many Russian manufacturers are worried by the impact of opening of the domestic market to foreign competition through the introduction of a single investment rate. Conversely, some directors, particularly the heads of the technology-intensive enterprises of the military industrial complex have set their hopes on the opening of the borders, with aims of participating in the world market.

C. *Executive and Legislative Power*

In the first half of 1992, splitting the power structures led inevitability to continual political crises, which is the social-political price to pay for the democratic implementation of economic reform.

Strong legislative power in the near future seems improbable. The worsening of the economic situation and sharpening of all social burdens caused by economic reform are inevitably accompanied by the rise (the "re-rise") of authoritarian tendencies: first, because the lack of consensus in society is reflected in parliament, and second, because of the necessity to concentrate power for quickly making important political decisions. However, the growth of authoritarianism does not mean the rejection of democracy. The latter will occur only if the extremist forces of national-patriotic orientation come to power, such as those now united with the neo-communist (bolshevik) opposition. A more probable--and much stronger--regime is the one ironically personified and based on democratic procedures, expressing long-term interests of societal development.

For concentration of power and authoritarianism do not necessarily mean total centralization of power. Under the "democratic option," power is concentrated in the hands of a leader and re-distributed along the whole management chain from top to bottom. On the other hand, under the tough nationalist-communist regime, one may expect Russia's splitting into separate regions, a consequence of regional leaders' desires to keep distance from the central power in both the political and economic spheres.

During the coming year the question concerning the character of Russian authoritarianism must be clarified. In the situation when we have two equal keepers of legitimate power (parliament and the President), there is a legal possibility to concentrate all power in the hands of the President. From this point of view, deciding the procedure for forming a government will be an important step on the way of forming an entire new political regime.

D. *Formation of Political Forces*

One of the distinguishing features of the current reform implementation is the fact that it is being carried out against a backdrop of a weak state and weakly structured society. The coming years will probably see strengthening of both, but not simultaneously, which will be a further source of tension and political crises.

For a long time, parties, in the old sense of the word, will not play an independent role in influencing the political processes. The same could be said about trade union structures (both traditional and newly-formed). Instead, they are all likely to be used for achieving political aims by those forces which are actually able to influence economic life and political decision making, which will in all likelihood be those directly connected with managerial and economic life.

By the middle of 1992 three centers of political force had come into being. First of all, there is a nationalistic bloc, which unites steadfast advocates of Russia's "special way" ideology and includes a wide range of organizations--from orthodox-communist to right-nationalist. Having a definite impact on the population and rather large representation in the parliament, this group will find it almost impossible to assert power--as opposed to influence--by constitutional methods. However, it is very unstable, as it does not accept the current course and it has no positive program, but rather finds sustenance through the population's perception of a non-stop increase of social burdens. It is very dangerous because it can coopt conservative forces among militarized groups and create a situation when their seizure of power by force could be justified.

At the opposite end of the spectrum, the "reformist team," relying in parliament on the most radically oriented deputies, has proved that it is able to participate actively in political life and--despite all the difficulties--can achieve its political targets. Its primary support is found in the organizations of Democratic Russia, which are very loyal to the President. This bloc is a radical free-market one, i.e., it relies on the ideas of economic liberalism.

Finally, today a force is coming into being which, under favorable conditions in the near future, will turn out to be a party of moderate-market (social-liberal) orientation. First of all, it includes the "Civil Union," uniting the "Renovation Union" (closely connected with the Russian Union of Manufacturers and Businessmen--A.I. Volsky, A.P. Vladislavlev), the Democratic Party of Russia (N.I. Travkin), the People's Party of Free Russia (A.V. Rutskoi) and a number of other organizations and factions. Uniting a large segment part of high officials, intelligentsia and those heads of state-owned enterprises who do not fully accept the tough market reform course, this party under certain developments could become an acceptable political alternative to market radicalism.

However, such a positive development of events will be possible only after the market changes have gone sufficiently far and the situation in Russia has become irreversible in economic and political respects. It is only then that one could speak about actual formation of a two-party system in the country, with radicals represented on both sides (their parliamentary representation will depend on special features of the election law).

2. Macroeconomic Trends in Economic Development

G.O. Kuranov
O.I. Izryadnova
A.V. Chernyavskaya

A. *Policy and Economic Marketing*

The following groups of factors influenced the development of the macroeconomic situation in the summer of 1992:

- factors of long-term character, including the structural deformity and technological backwardness of the production process, extensive methods used in the national economy and preservation of large non-productive legacies (national defense, social programs, and foreign assistance);

- factors that developed actively during the Gorbachev "destroying" period, directed at restructuring of the old structures;

- factors connected simultaneously with liberalization and with the tough stabilization policy at the beginning of the radical reforms; and

- factors connected with correcting the reform policy in the spring and summer of 1992 (low interest credit for industry, softening the fiscally restrictive budget policy, reform of foreign economic activities).

If the first group of factors mainly exacerbated existing long-term crisis trends, which lead neither to any noticeable rise nor to a fast fall in production, the others had a more immediate impact on macroeconomic processes. The collapse of the "planning-managing" structures, adding to socio-political instability, centrifugal tendencies and political ambition, has accelerated the sense of general economic failure, most specifically in the financial and currency sectors. It has created a threat of impending economic crash.

On the one hand, decisive stabilization and liberalization measures have helped the government avoid budgetary collapse and remove the suffocating "money overhang" while at the same time fighting hyperinflation. The financial situation could return to "normal"-- but only at the cost of big reductions in aggregate demand and a slowing down of investment activity. On the other hand, the producers' inadequate response to the market conditions has resulted in a new crisis--a huge increase of mutual debts, which might be considered a kind of non-monetary reaction to monetary pressures.

The producers' behavior, in view of sharply changed management practice and tough budget and credit constraints, has led by necessity to development of corrective tactics. In second quarter 1992, one could observe a loosening of financial and monetary policy. At the same time, paradoxically, price liberalization has continued. The rise of wholesale and retail prices became permanent and was accompanied by a general fall of production in practically all branches and by a decrease in business and investment activities.

The fall in production was initiated by the destruction of traditional ties of cooperation in Russia itself and also within the CIS and the Baltic countries. Increasing expense burdens are shifting onto regions that are predominantly consumers of finished products. This worsens economic relations already strained by the introduction of new national currencies and money substitutes in the territory of the ruble zone.

With prices and interest rates rising sharply, the introduction of a new taxation practice at enterprises turned out to be insufficient to implement normal capital replacement processes. The violations of contract and payment discipline, which earlier were compensated by administrative methods, resulted under conditions of management liberalization in a liquidity crisis. The clearing system changed with the introduction of regional clearing houses in late 1991, but they function poorly, are unable to provide timely payments and have only sharpened the payments crisis. The price changes were not coordinated with the volume of money and other means of payments, affecting the investment and consumption spheres.

As the enterprises suffer from shortages of their own means, they have to curtail capital construction (quite unprecedented for the Russian economy) and use profits to satisfy the current non-productive consumption of the workers. Meanwhile, profit in real terms has continued to drop. In April-May, it decreased even in nominal terms--by 11% and 25%, respectively, whereas wholesale prices in industry rose by 28% and 17%. The pricing policy of enterprises and the payments crisis are both explained by the impossibility of changing in a relatively short time the stereotypic behavior of producers who have been traditionally sure of state guardianship; moreover, one could witness a sharp lag in institutional and economic structural transformation, without which macroeconomic stabilization effects cannot be sustained.

All this is complicated by the strong influence on the economic situation exercised by the price increase in fuel and energy resources, especially because inflation expectations are affected both in the field of production and consumption.

Another important influence on the character of economic development can be seen in the introduction of the single ruble rate to the dollar and adjustment of accounts of enterprises and the state according to the results of their foreign trade activity.

B. _Production_

National income produced in Russia decreased in January-July 1992 by 18% compared with the corresponding period of the previous year (Table 1). The decline in net production volume can be observed in all branches of the national economy, and has been accompanied by a further decrease of effectiveness of production resource use and also by the outstripping growth of production expenses compared with profits. Because of foreign trade turnover limitation and irrational economic losses, the resources of the national income used for consumption and capital accumulation are decreasing. Preliminary estimates of consumed national income volume show a 27% decline (including a 17% drop in consumption and a 50% drop in accumulation).

One of the main features of the present economic crisis is a relatively large decline in production of finished goods, as characterized by the information given in Table 2.

Between January and August of this year, industrial production decreased by 16.6% compared with the same period of 1991 (in June 14.6%, July 21%, August 27.2%). The production of consumer goods from February to July decreased by 15% as compared with last year (non-food products 10%; 17% in June, 21.5% in July).

Slackening of production in all sectors of the national economy and its regions leads to a further decline of investment activity. The sharp limitation on budgetary financing of capital investments, a considerable increase in the price of building materials and services, imbalance between building sites material and technological maintainance capacity, and sky rocketing interest rates have resulted in cutting down construction programs in both production and non-production spheres. The uncertainty of the economic situation, especially concerning privatization, acts as a brake on attempts to stimulate production at the level of viable enterprise. Given technological backwardness in most branches, cutting down investment activity may have irreversible consequences.

For the first six months of the present year, capital investment volume in the national economy from all sources was down 46% in prices comparable with the prices of the same period last year. The main reasons were a decline of amortization funds as the source of investments, a fall in long-term credit due to virtually negative real interest rates, and both the enterprises' own preferences to use money for current consumption before it loses its value and lack of interest in any long-term investments (which in the short run decrease the financial resources left at the enterprises' disposal). The volume of centralized investments within the first six months of 1992 was down by 34.2%.

C. *Prices and Goods Turnover*

The retail turnover of state and cooperative trade from January to July was only 60% of the previous year's level. The growing gap between the rates of decrease in consumer goods production and increase in turnover is explained by great retail prices growth, which is outstripping income growth, and also by the development of barter.

As a result of wide-scale price liberalization, the index of retail prices and tariffs paid on services to the population compared with corresponding period of the previous year grew in July 8.3 times, and in February-July 6.3 times. The price of services provided to the population in February-June grew 6 times, and in July they increased a further 31%. The index of retail prices in July compared with June rose 107.4%.

The sharp rise of retail prices is mainly determined by the level of wholesale prices in industry and purchase prices in agriculture. The index of the wholesale prices of industrial producers (without VAT) in February-July 1992 compared with the same period last year was up 15.7 times; the purchase prices in agricultural production grew 5.4 times. The dynamics of industrial wholesale prices for January-April slowed somewhat from month to month, but in May-June there was a steep rise due to administratively increased prices on energy and fuel. The total price rise in June compared with May was 36%.

The dynamics of prices reflects the traditionally established structure of production priorities. Prices in mining industry production and production connected with the initial processing of mineral and fuel raw materials grew much faster than in production of final products. The one exception was in fuels: the price index of electric power and fuel industry products was lower than the general one in industry; however, May's introduction of the new regulated prices of energy-producing products changed the ratio somewhat. The wholesale prices of processing products grew June an average 2.9 times, including gasoline 3 to 3.5 times, diesel fuel 2.8 to 3.6 times, mazut (black oil) 2.4 to 3.8 times. In June, the price rise in electric power engineering was 1.9 times, in oil and gas industry 3.2 times, in coal industry 3.9 times.

In other branches of industry, the price rise in May and June was up an average 15%-16%, not yet reflecting the energy price rise impact. In July, the average price rise was 17%, and in August 13%.

The situation in monetary circulation in January-June was strained and difficult: there was still the tendency of household incomes to outstrip expenditures. Since the beginning of the year, one can observe a diminishing gap between the population's incomes and expenditures. Incomes within the January-July 1992 period increased 6.2 times over the corresponding 1991 period, but expenditures increased only 5.2 times. The monetary incomes growth, not supported by a commensurately growing supply of goods and services, has intensified the tendency to amass money in a forced way and reduce the speed of velocity of money, which increases the turmoil in the financial system. In March, due to increased social payments and wages, the excess of incomes over expenditures was 73% higher than in February, and in April it was 50% more than it had been in March, all of which resulted in a further increase in the amount of money in the population's possession, and was accompanied by an additional emission of money, growing to a total of 459.5 billion rubles in July.

One can observe a process of labor pay naturalization ("pay in kind"), which, together with "barterization" of economic mutual ties and settlement systems among enterprises without bank structures, aggravates the negative processes of the monetary circulation.

D. *RF Foreign Trade in the Summer of 1992*

The dynamics of foreign trade development within the first six months of 1992 are shown in Table 3.

During the two summer months of 1992, Russian foreign trade was characterized by a certain stabilization of exports (on the level of $3 billion) and there was after February a leap in imports equal to $4.2 billion, which can be mainly explained by the growth of massive food purchases with help of foreign credits.

Against the background of a continuous decline of the main indices, one could notice that this process somewhat slowed in July 1992 (Table 4). As a result, June's foreign trade balance was favorable (albeit about $300 million less than in the previous year); in July, though, it was negative, exceeding $1 billion (last July, it was equal to zero).

The slowdown of decline in exports in July was due to increasing exports of energy resources, primarily natural gas (Table 5). That produced an even more considerable shift in the structure of Russian exports into energy. Thus, their proportion in total exports reached 48% in January to June, and 52% in January to July.

The increase of imports to the Russian Federation in July 1992 was chiefly conditioned by an increase in the purchase of grain and medicines on new credits. The rate of increase in purchasing grain, however, is less now than it was in previous months (Table 6). The tendency is likely to remain, and will be perhaps accelerated in the autumn and winter of 1992 by changing conditions in the grant of new credits (including American ones) for promotion of agricultural produce. These changes will bring about an increase in purchase of meat and meat-based products.

With the help of credits, a decrease in the import of machines and equipment has managed to slow. As a result, their proportion in total imports amounted to 34% between January and July, compared with 25% between January and May.

No substantial changes in the geographic structure of Russian foreign trade occurred in summer of 1992. The share of individualized and industrializing capitalist countries has expanded to cover 72%-73% of the total import volume. Compared with the same period of 1991, their proportion in the volume of Russian foreign trade has risen by seven percentage points. Due to an economic crisis and also to the fact that all mutual payments are effected now in hard currency, the volume of trade of most of the former socialist countries has dropped to the lowest indices.

In June 1992, Russia's foreign debt totaled $74.3 billion (Russian State Statistics Committee data); accrued interest reached $50.3 billion.

E. *Macroeconomic Forecast for 1992*

The primary conditions determining macroeconomic tendencies in the second half of 1992 and into 1993 are as follows:

1. A slowing down in the rise of wholesale and retail prices and tariffs: As has been pointed out, new wholesale prices of oil are expected to be at the level of 30%-35% of the world market prices. This will probably bring about a 40%-45% rise in average price index, and, taking into account all factors, possibly up to 70%-75%. This estimation takes into consideration May-June rises in prices of fuel and other energy-related material and also a predicted moderate credit emission correlated with the growth of demand for circulating capital assets. Further price rises due to fuel and energy price liberalization could reach 5%-10% per month.

2. Moderate credit emission, which is necessary to cover the debts of industrial enterprises: It should be remembered that solvency problems are just another manifestation of structural and industrial crisis and cannot be solved by means of crediting debt balances and introducing bill of exchange registration. At the same time, if these problems are not

overcome by means of restructuring the economy, they will give rise to continual credit emission, which will be the source of the constant component of inflation.

3. It is expected that there will be revision of privileges--including export taxation--given earlier to some industrial sectors and a considerable number of Russian regions concerning their foreign trade, as a result of which the budget was not replenished by considerable currency receipts in the first half of the year. Under conditions of further foreign trade liberalization and abolition of export quotas and licenses (except quotas for energy and strategic raw materials), all the producers and regions should be treated equally. With transition to ruble convertability, obligatory sale by exporters of 50% of currency receipts at market rate, and required full-ruble coverage for the import of material and technical resources and credits, mass subsidy on import through different ruble rates can be abolished. Beside centralized purchase of corn and foodstuffs, subsidies will be preserved for imported foodstuffs for children, medicines and medical equipment, raw materials for food production, some types of chemical raw materials, and equipment for the agricultural complex. The volume of budget subsidies, depending on the variations of products, will be between 400 billion-900 billion rubles.

It is assumed that as a result of transition to ruble convertability, the import of machinery equipment and chemical industry will immediately be reduced, and delivery of raw materials for chemical and light industry and some products of centralized import for population (including foodstuffs) will be considerably lowered.

4. Funds revalued on July 1 (stipulated by RF Government), and their subsequent regular (every six months) revaluation and indexation will help enlarge the deprecation fund

31

and make it the leading source of financing. Other funds will come from investment tax credit. Further on, additional sources of investment will be found in the private savings of the population, pension funds and medical insurance funds. As a result, it can be expected that the rapid decrease in investment activity will slow by the beginning of 1993, and general investment volume will eventually reach the level of 1992.

It should be noted that in 1992 investment recession will be about 50% of the 1991 level. None of macroeconomic indices reveals such a lowering. The capital accumulation share of the national income which formed 25%-27% in 1985-86, dropped in 1990 to 21%, and in 1991 to 14%. Its further fall--to 10%-12%--is expected in 1992.

5. Due to the institutional reform and speeding-up of privatization process, one can expect greater activity in medium and small business as well as agriculture in 1993. Civil goods production will grow at converted military enterprises, and contraction of food and consumer goods production will slow down.

Most importantly, however, short-term perspectives in the development of Russia's economic situation depend on decisions in the sphere of refinancing the chain of debts of state enterprises to each other and "pseudocommercial" bank structures.

Given current tendencies in the retrenchment of production, national income by the end of 1992 will be reduced by at least 20%. The varying scales of production and consumption can be brought closer, depending on how mutual debts of enterprises are abolished and on the dynamics of wage and salary income growth. The same concerns the dynamics of gross national product (GNP), defined as ultimate utilization. But if the present discrepancy between demand and availability of payment continues until the end of the year, the drop in consumed national income and GNP will be as high as 40%.

In general, a certain slowing down in industrial production contraction is expected by the fourth quarter of 1992. Recession will have probably reached its lowest point (up to 22%-25%) in summer and autumn. Recession in industry will reach, by some estimations, 17%-18% in 1992, and 8%-10% in 1993.

The share of the fuel-energy complex and forestry in the structure of industrial production will grow, while that of metallurgy, mechanical engineering, and chemistry will continue to shrink.

Taking into consideration the dynamics of material expenditures and net national product, gross domestic output will decrease in 1992 by 20%-21% and in 1993 by a further 7%-9%, and individual consumption will decline by 17%. The relative share of accumulation will gradually grow, which is the most obvious symptom of overcoming the crisis.

Stabilizing the Russian economy (i.e., reaching the lowest point of recession) can be expected by 1995-1996. If national income and GNP grow steadily by 3%-4% in the following years, 1990 levels in macroindices will be reached by 2005-2006. Such a scenario, though, presupposes a return to the national income structure of the end of the 1980s, preservation of the most important economic ties between CIS countries, and broad deployment of foreign investment (calculations show that domestic accumulation resources are not enough for the state to overcome the crisis).

I.V. Kolsnitsin

F. *Income and Consumer Demand of Population*

In the second quarter of the year, particularly in May and June, the processes of inflationary income rise continued; incomes of the population rose by 36%, coming to 369.3 billion rubles in June. The gap between income and expenses also increased; in the first half-year it was 19.4% of total income, but by July it came to 49.5%. Table 7 shows the dynamics of income and expenses of the population in 1991-92.

It should be stressed, however, that in *real* terms the imbalance between income and expenses was only 25% of what it had been of the end of 1991 (not reflected in the table). Therefore, the situation of the consumer market in summer 1992 is substantially less tense than it was at the end of last year. The nominal increase in savings is caused by the consumption restructuring rather than by the "absolute" lack of goods and services.

The average monthly salary has increased 7.3 times as compared with the first half of 1991, becoming 2,880 rubles. The salary growth continued all during the period, reaching 39% in February, 12% in April, 20% in May and 19% in June. The average salary in June was estimated to be approximately 4,400 rubles.

By June, the disproportion which was formed during the first half-year of 1992 was on the whole eliminated. The only thing which remained is the somewhat higher salary differentiation in industry as compared with national economy in general (117% compared to 106%-107% in the first two quarters of 1991).

G. *Consumer Demand of the Population*

Because of the drastic fall of people's solvency in the first six months, a certain balance between supply and demand was achieved, accompanied by a decrease in real terms in sales (commodity turnover volume). In the first half-year in general there was not any stable tendency shown in the changes of commodity turnover volume, as illustrated by the data given in Table 8.

Thus, after the January commodity turnover "flop," in subsequent months this index returned into a "stable" regime, and the average value for January-March coincided with the average quarter level for the second quarter (93.5 billion rubles). The macrostructure commodity turnover index (proportion of foodstuffs and non-foodstuffs in the turnover structure) changed through an increase of foodstuffs in the total volume turnover. While in December the sale of foodstuffs was only 37% of the total turnover (calculation was made on the basis of price statistics) and in January the proportion of both types of commodities was equal, in the subsequent months the foodstuff portion became even higher than 50% (according to our estimates by 2-3 percentage points). It should be noted that until the mid-1980s the share of manufactured goods grew in the general commodity structure. Thus, the dynamics of the index in question reflect indirectly that there is a grave crisis in the consumption market.

Increase in nominal incomes and the process of restructuring consumer demand was, unfortunately, accompanied by a drastic fall in production of consumer goods. In the first half-year foodstuff production, for instance, decreased by 23% as compared with the same period of the previous year. The most sharp fall production was in meat, cereals, and pastries (by 27%-35%), while fish production declined by half.

As a result, consumption of the following goods decreased compared with 1991: milk products by 25%, meat by 15%, fish by 17%. Fruits and berries consumption declined by more than by half, tomatoes by 34%, cucumbers by 40%, and cabbages by 71%.

In July, unfavorable tendencies in the animal husbandry production market remained due to a persistent wide gap between price demands of producers and people's solvency. During the first week of July alone, meat and whole milk production decreased 20% and 6%, respectively. According to forecasts for 1992, total meat and milk production will probably decrease by no less than 20% and 40%, respectively.

In general, the consumer demand became more active in July, provoked partly by grave inflationary expectations. Preliminary data have shown that the commodity turnover had risen approximately by 3% (in comparable prices).

According to experts' estimates, during the first half of 1992 the availability of foodstuffs increased, and was at its highest in July (in Moscow and St. Petersburg, physical availability of foodstuffs was the highest in June and somewhat decreased in August). Naturally, the economic availability of the product was determined by the balance between the income increase and price growth, which has decreased approximately three times as compared with December 1991.

H. *Retail Prices*

The first six months of 1992 can be characterized as a period of both drastic increase in price level and change in price structure. The dynamics of consumer price index (CPI) is illustrated by the data given in Table 9.

In January, foodstuff prices grew faster (the CPI for this group was twice as high as for paying services and 1.5 times as for manufactured goods). Later, however, the CPI goods grew quicker, its growth in February-March was about 25 percentage points higher than the price index for foodstuffs. In May-June both indices were characterized by similar dynamics (they constituted 111%-113%); in July the CPI for services became a "leader" (the July index as compared with June was 140%). Probably, in the third quarter the inflationary increase in expense will cause even quicker growth of foodstuffs CPI, and the demand constraints (if they to some extent retain their present importance) will for a certain period of time play a role of a suppressing factor in case of manufactured goods price growth.

In Russia a considerable territorial differentiation of the retail price index (which is slightly different statistically from CPI) was observed in 1992. Thus, whereas the price index in June 1992 as compared with June 1991 was 912 nationwide, in Tatarstan it was 753 and in Voronež 754, but in the Saha (Yakutiya) Republic it was 1,315.

The prices of certain major groups of consumer goods have grown unevenly. In January, prices of the most important foodstuffs (milk, sugar, salt, vegetable, oil, some sorts of bread) remained at the administratively fixed maximum level. Since the first half of February, when local budget funds for subsidies were exhausted, prices have risen gradually. In

March, the foodstuffs price rise was mainly in those goods whose prices were initially limited; free prices did not change fundamentally.

According to the Government Committee on Statistics (GKS), milk prices were still regulated in 40% of towns by the end of June, rye bread prices were regulated in 30%, and wheat bread prices were fixed in 32%. Price regulation was most common in the towns of the Volga Region, Volgo-Viatsk and Northern Economic Regions.

Table 10, using data furnished by the Independent Research Center "Contur" FASPI, shows the real increase picture in the value of the Russian consumer basket (consisting of 15 goods: meat, sausage, vegetable oil, butter, fats, milk, sugar, eggs, bread, flour, pastry, salt, vodka, tobacco).

Prices in Moscow and St. Petersburg were approximately 20% higher than the average. The difference between independent estimates and the GKS index was substantial: from 200% in January to 186% in June.

Although the rise in foodstuffs CPI slowed in the second quarter of the year, the continued price increase turned out to be painful for the population. The average price of a man's suit has grown 600%, while a woman's suit cost 520% more, the price of a color TV set has jumped 740% and a refrigerator cost 1,600% more than at the beginning of the year. Children's goods went up more than 10 times in price during the first half-year.

As mentioned, service prices grew faster in the second quarter than did other prices. The consumer price index for services exceeded 600 as compared with December and came up to 140 as compared with the previous month. While the payment for kindergartens and nurseries grew 1,200%-1,400% during the six months, sanatorium-resort and health services grew at least as drastically, in certain regions as much as 2,000%.

The processes going on in the sphere of price formation cause progressive deterioration of the consumption structure (the hypergrowth of the goods component in expenses), prevent most consumers from following any rational models of behavior, and distort signals going into the industrial sphere.

The data obtained by the GKS Department of Social Statistics confirm the general conclusion of the unfavorable changes taking place in the consumption structure of households. In May-June, when the share of foodstuffs (including alcohol) was about 50% of all consumer expenditures, the share of services decreased to 10.9% (Table 11). The manufactured goods increase in the total volume of expenses, inevitable after the initial "price jump," has been extremely sluggish ever since. Whereas in 1991 foodstuff expenditures equalled 75% of total non-foodstuff expenditures, by May-June 1992 they totaled 103.6% of the latter.

3. The State of Government Budget and Government Tax Policy

S.G. Sinelnikov-Murylev
L.I. Anisimova

A new budget system in Russia continues developing in 1992, as only this year the government finance system began to attempt the entire range of budgetary functions of an independent state. It has resulted in radical changes in the structure of government revenues and expenditures. In the current year, revenue is supposed to reach 40.8% of the GNP, while expenditure will be 45.5% of the GNP (Table 12).

Massive transformation in the revenue and expenditure structures of the federal and local budgets in Russia has also taken place: in 1990, local budget revenues made up about 82% of the central budget and in 1991 93%, but in 1992 dropped to 63%. Due to the concentration of governmental finance deficit in the federal budget, local budgets' expenditures, which had equalled 82% of federal budget expenditure in 1990, fell to 73% in 1991, and to 49% in 1992.

Unstable economic development has forced a systematic adjustment of the basic characteristics of Russia's budget system. The draft budget for the first quarter of 1992 assumed that revenues and expenditures would be balanced, through heavy taxation. The law "On Adjusting the Russian Federation Budget System Indicators for the First Quarter of 1992" provided for a federal budget deficit of 64.7 billion rubles, or 5.8% of Russia's forecast GNP.

In the first quarter of 1992, the federal budget deficit was 4.7 billion rubles, although expenditures of 45.8 billion rubles planned for the first quarter were not financed until April 1992. Thus, the federal budget deficit in the first quarter can be assessed at 50.5 billion rubles (about 3.6% of the GNP). With a significant shortfall in revenue in the consolidated budget, such results may be explained by the expenditure partial performance at only 85% of the adjusted plan.

The federal budget deficit in the first half of 1992 was 301.1 billion rubles, or about 7.5% of the GNP. Central Bank of Russia credits of 282.5 billion rubles were used to cover the bulk of the deficit. In the local budgets' performance over the first half of the year, revenues exceeded expenditures by 85.4 billion rubles.

In July 1992 the federal budget deficit grew by 64%, to 492.9 billion rubles, or 9.9% of the GNP. Over eight months, the federal budget deficit, as estimated, accounted for 820 billion rubles (about 13.5% of GNP). The Central Bank of Russia borrowed funds amounting to 935.5 billion rubles. This may be explained both by the shortfall in revenue and the increase in government expenditures. For the first half of 1992, expenditures in the national economy grew to 9.6% of GNP, and by the end of July made up 11%. Social spending grew from 7.4% of the GNP in the first quarter of 1992 to 8.4% over the first seven months of 1992; defense expenditures grew from 4.25% to 5.8% of the GNP; government administration expenditures on law-enforcement bodies increased from 1.9% to 2.3% of the GNP.

The indicated budget growth is caused to a great extent by the seasonal character of some economic processes, by the need to grant credit for agricultural production, and delivery of food to the polar region.

In view of the price rise in energy sources in May 1992 and the introduction of supplementary social security measures, the 1992 draft budget was reconsidered. In July, the Russian Federation bill "On the Budget System of Russian Federation for 1992" was passed, followed by the Supreme Soviet resolution putting it into effect (the budget basic indicators are given in Table 12).

The approved budget is a compromise between the Russian government, which proposed that consolidated budget and expenditure revenue be equal at 4.4 trillion rubles, and the parliament, which assumed both budget revenue and expenditure would be increased. The budget revenue was increased by 130 billion rubles, the expenditure by 454.5 billion rubles over the original government draft budget. Moreover, the bill provides for increasing federal budget expenditure by 334.2 billion rubles (more than 2% of GNP) in the event extra receipts are obtained.

According to the law adopted, the consolidated budget deficit in 1992 is 640.2 billion rubles (including foreign economic credit in the sum of 91 billion rubles) or 4% of GNP, which is forecast at 15.5 trillion rubles. For the first seven months of 1992, the overall expenditure on national economy is due to be 11.8% of GNP; for the year as a whole, it is expected to decline to 7.2%. Social security expenses remain at the same level, defense expenses are supposed to be cut by 2 percentage points of GNP, and overall administrative expenses by 0.3 points of GNP.

Table 13 shows Russia's government finance receipts over the first quarter of 1992, the first half of 1992 and over the whole year 1992 (forecast). Besides the consolidated budget revenue, the estimates include the receipts of non-budget items and pension funds, as well as government revenues from purchasing at an overvalued exchange rate--0.018 dollar/ruble--some of the hard currency earnings of export manufacturers during the first half of the year. Government receipts in the first quarter made up about 38% of GNP, 36% in the first half, and is forecast to rise to 42% for the whole year.

Tables 14 and 15 cite figures on tax returns in the Russia's budget over the first seven months of 1992. Russia's tax system for the present is not able to ensure a stable budget revenue rise that would be in line with the gross domestic product nominal volume increase; in May and June, tax revenue growth rate lagged significantly behind GNP growth. If we consider the dynamics of both monthly tax rates and GNP, we shall see the lag in March as well. As a result, budget tax revenue in proportion to GNP was rather unstable. This is caused by both tax revenue fluctuations owed to the existing tax-payment procedure and its corrections, and by nominal GNP volume dynamics.

Profit tax revenue over the seven months of 1992 made up 39% of the total revenue in the consolidated budget. In April, a sharp rise in the budget receipts on profit tax took place, due to the resettlement of payments on the basis of real profit gained in the first quarter. Extra payments amounted to 63 billion rubles. A more than twofold increase in tax returns in July against those in June might be explained in the same way. Table 16 shows the monthly dynamics of profit over the national economy.

At present, the rate of the real withdrawals of profit from enterprises is influenced on one hand by tax benefits to enterprises (about 160 billion rubles in the first six months of 1992, or 11.8% of the pretax profit), and on the other by the wage growth rate against changes in regulated payment for labor included in cost pricing. The interaction between these factors led to a near doubling in the pretax profit withdrawals rate, from 17% in the first quarter of 1992 to almost 33% for the first half year 1992.

In January-July, value-added tax returns accounted for 29% of the overall budget revenue, while excise taxes counted for about 4%. The drop in growth rates on excise taxes and VAT receipts in the second quarter of 1992 was caused by the deep crisis in the enterprises' ability to pay. According to Russian Federation State Tax Service information for the six months, the budget did not receive VAT returns at over 300 billion rubles because of delayed end-consumer payment to manufacturers. Meanwhile, personal income tax brings only 8.6% of Russia's budget revenue.

A number of regions introduced taxes and fees that are not envisaged by Russian laws. Thus, according to the State Tax Service, the Daghestan SSR, Sakha Republic, Buryatiya, Krasnoyarsk Territory, Irkutsk, Nizhny Novgorod, Saratov, Sverdlovsk and Amur Regions have introduced natural resources fees; the Kabardino-Balkarsk SSR, Krasnoyarsk Territory and Nizhny Novgorod Region have introduced transport duties, fishing and hunting duties, and, among others, fees for allotting land for constructing industrial objects.

In addition, some regions have passed resolutions on transfer of federal taxes into local budgets. Thus, the Sakha Republic fixed VAT and profit tax charges to the local budget at 100% in the first quarter of 1992. In the second quarter, instead of the profit tax, the republic introduced its own enterprises' income tax, which is not sent to the federal budget. However, only one-fifth of Russia Federation territory has passed resolutions on local taxes. The Supreme Soviet's resolution voids decisions passed in a number of regions about transfer of the federal budget receipts to their budgets. The resolution allows the government and the central bank to suspend, when necessary, financing enterprises, to stop export licensing, to suspend food supplies from state resources, and to control state bank credit rates and money emission. The resolution gives instructions to the Ministry of Finance and the State Tax Service of Russian Federation to keep double control on performance of laws in force.

In summer 1992, further changes in Russia's tax system occurred. The government resolution "On the Government Regulation of the Price on Energy Resources and Other Goods and Services," adopted in May 1992, introduces payments based on output from oil and gas producing enterprises to the Price Regulation Fund. Charges for prices exceeding regulated limits are also levied to the fund. The Russian Federation law "On Mineral Wealth" introduces special duties on the use of mineral resources.

In June 1992, a number of resolutions concerning taxation were adopted by the Supreme Soviet, as well as the law "On Alterations and Additions to the Russia's Tax System." According to the resolution adopted, the procedure of calculating and levying of profit tax, VAT, and income tax is significantly changed.

In the sphere of profit taxation, a range of benefits for enterprises has been changed. From July 1, in every industry, enterprises are allowed to deduct the value of expenses for technical re-equipment from taxable profit. Enterprises with a foreign capital share operating in the sphere of material production which were registered before January 1, 1992 preserve the tax holidays that release them from paying profit tax during the first two years after pretax profit is received. In addition, profit repaid for state-targeted credits used for working capital is tax deductible.

Due to inflation, on August 8, 1992 it was decided to revalue fixed assets to ensure proper conditions for their replacement. To implement the resolution, all the enterprises and organizations on the territory of Russia, irrespective of the forms of ownership, were to revalue their fixed assets. The procedure of revaluation is as follows: a renewal value of fixed assets is calculated on the basis of initial book value multiplied by a fixed recalculation coefficient that differs depending on the asset type and the date of its acquisition. For fixed assets acquired before 1991, the coefficient varies from 4.5 to 46, while for those acquired in 1991 from 3 to 20; assets acquired in 1992 are not subject to revaluation.

From January 1, 1993, VAT rates will be reduced up to 10% on food (except excised, such as in the case of vodka) and children's goods, and up to 20% on other goods.

Rates of allocation from federal taxes into territorial budgets changed, too. At present 20% of VAT, enterprise profit tax at the rate of 19% (59.4% of earnings), 50% of income figured from excise profits on alcohol, and 100% of other federal excises (except those on motor-cars) are included there. In order to reduce local budget subsidies, the law "On the Budget System for 1992" established 25% and 30% shares of VAT allocations for separate territories.

In the law "On the Personal Income Taxation," where numerous amendments concerning the way of calculation of taxable income were made, scale indexation and progressive rates start from 200,000 rubles, not from 42,000 rubles, as previously.

4. Financial Problems of the Economy

S.N. Zhuravlev
A. Ivanov
A. Komarov

A. *Monetary Sector*

By the beginning of the second half of 1992, which coincides with the start of reforms, a new macroeconomic situation which may be briefly described as "money acquires more and more significance, but becomes less controllable," was gradually taking shape. This situation was characterized by the following three peculiarities.

Demand For Money

It is possible now to speak about a certain stabilization in the demand for money and its circulation speed. This fact fundamentally changes the role of money in the economy in comparison with the first "post-liberalization" period, which directly followed price liberalization (January-May 1992).

From April-May enterprise monetary balances reached their "bottom" and for a very long period stood still at a rather low point (about 12%-15% of the "pre-liberalization" level). In principal, such a sharp decrease is consistent with growth of the "alternative cost of keeping money" (measured by the nominal interest and by the expected inflation), which is why it is hardly possible to forecast its growth in the near future.

As for the most liquid monetary units, such as balance on hand in the consumer market, the stabilization of the money demand may be forecast with much more certainty (because the speed of its circulation which continued to rise before the beginning of spring 1992, then began to lower little by little, and to the middle of summer 1992, practically reached the "normal" level, corresponding to the perennial trend). It is a signal of the filling of money in the "cash niche," formed as a result of the January hyperinflation correction. From this fact it is possible to draw the rather unpleasant conclusion that, if during the period April-June 1992 the main mass of money in cash emission "fell" into this niche without causing additional inflation, during the next months the emission rate will most probably directly determine price rises at the consumer level.

By the beginning of summer 1992, the amount of money in circulation started to influence economic processes, mainly price movement, although the effect of the money supply on the real economy is only just beginning to take place. The national economy is not yet "market" enough to launch the standard mechanisms of such influence (both the Keynesian--i.e., through the influence of interest rates on investments--and the monetarist--i.e., through the errors on inflationary expectations caused by shifts in the money supply). One, however, cannot say whether it is good or bad.

Money Supply

a. Monetary Base

Since the period April-June 1992, such factors as assets for mutual payments between the states of the ruble zone and the growing deficit of the federal budget have been influencing the money supply itself. These factors cannot be controlled by the Central Bank of Russia. By the beginning of the third quarter of 1992, the money supply had almost lost its role as an autonomous variable. By this time, the only central bank instrument to regulate the amount of money supply--the refinancing of commercial banks--had also lost its role.

The financial policy of the government is undergoing curious changes. In the beginning of 1992, when the economic stabilization was not determined by the state of the budget (a shock increase in prices in January 1992 led to price level stabilization in the next 2-3 months), the state of the budget was the focus of attention. Nowadays, when the budget deficit directly determines the inflation rate, the cutting of the government expenditures is a minor goal. It does not mean that the government is not aware of the current situation. Rather, it shows a new balance of forces in the government bodies exercising economic management which makes it more difficult to chose between stabilization of finances at the expense of industrial collapse and the preservation of the industrial potential at the expense of financial crisis (Tables 17, 18).

b. *Bank Reserves, a Multiplier and a Credit Potential*

By the end of summer 1992, the situation in the financial sphere was very much like a tightened spring: in the middle of May, the monetary base monthly growth rates were at the level of 50%. As far as prices were concerned, their growth rates by the middle of summer had stabilized and since then they have been behind money supply growth rates.

The indices of bank multiplication show how much the "monetary spring" is tightened. These indices characterize the rate of accumulating deposits by commercial banks (i.e., the ratio of deposit increase to reserve expansion). In the second quarter 1992, the indices went down, showing that banks had accumulated a large unrealized credit potential. The rate of the expansion of commercial banks' credits to enterprises was slower in the second quarter as compared with the first. Presumably, it became impossible to allocate all the potentially available credits at the high interest rates (though they were negative, in view of the expected yearly inflation rate of 500%-700%). Borrowers from commercial banks were more and more concentrated in the "hot sector" of commercial structures with a rather high level of profitability. The money supply growth rates were also lower than expected because of the lack of cash money.

Practice shows that this situation is very dangerous because of the invisible inflationary "ceiling" which is forming within the financial system. This "ceiling" began to fall at the end of August 1992, after the ruble depreciation in hard currency exchange had caused an increase in prices of imported commodities. This will soon lead to the increase in prices on domestic products. At the same time, and even earlier, the money supply growth rates, especially its most liquid components (i.e., cash holdings of the households and the money on the accounts of enterprises), almost reached the monetary base growth rates, which were rather high. The credit potential of commercial banks has continued to grow: during the first ten days of July their assets in their respective accounts in the central bank grew by 90 billion rubles, which exceeds the same index for the whole first quarter of 1992. As a result, one can forecast a rather high increase in the money supply, especially of its liquid components, which can directly influence the price level in the next months this year (Tables 19, 20).

B. *The Forecast of the Development in the Financial Sphere and Its Influence on the Economy in the Whole*

In accordance with obligations adopted by the government and the central bank, in the second half of 1992 the monetary base expansion will not exceed 1.5 billion rubles. The existing calculations show that the implementations of this goal would cause the doubling of the money supply during the first part of 1992, given an average monthly increase rate of 15%. This could bring the average monthly inflation rate down to the level of 6%-9% in the second part of 1992.

However, the real situation will presumably develop in another way. Rapid inflation, the result of monetization of the budget deficit, can be expected even without taking into consideration such factors as the expectations of production cost increases (caused by oil prices liberalization in September 1992 and transition to new prices on agricultural products) and the efforts of the central bank to settle the crisis of non-payments, which may cause the "printing" of at least 1 trillion rubles.

The budget income forecast is based on the dynamics of the total volume of industrial output and profits and incomes of the population, and also takes into consideration their relation with the different budget provisions. (To forecast budget expenses, the trends which had taken place by July 1992 were extrapolated for the end of the year (Table 21).

C. *Commercial Banks*

Credit Policy

Credits to enterprises and organizations amounted to 50% of aggregate balance sheets. The credit volume growth rate was slower than that of assets. This means that the share of credits has been reduced, from 54% on May 1 to 49% on July 1. Long-term credits amounted to 6% of the total sum of credits. Many banks have considerably reduced the volume of their credits. The reasons are the following:

First, inflation and the growing value of financial resources caused permanent increases of the interest rate.

Second, credit policy was influenced by the crisis of payments and the instability of the economic situation.

Third, the permanent changes made by the central bank in the obligatory terms of commercial bank operation have not encouraged long-term investments and have required that assets should be more liquid.

The Influence of Inflation on Commercial Bank Activity

One of the features of the operation of the central bank and commercial banks is negative interest rates in real terms (with the inflation taken into consideration). Despite the widespread view that the credits are very expensive, they are in fact given at negative interest rates. It is impossible to achieve a real interest rate (although it was defined as one of the major goals of the central bank), because even credits with such negative rates are too expensive for state-owned enterprises whose assets are depreciating even more rapidly.

There is no indexation of current assets. Prices on equipment grew ten times, whereas depreciation rates remained unchanged. As a result, the enterprises cannot replace their fixed assets with their own funds. It is obvious that under these conditions the only way for enterprises to maintain their viability is to use cheap credit and mutual credit in the form of overdue debts.

Certain measures have been taken by commercial banks to save their resources from inflationary depreciation. Some commercial banks invested their capital in acquisition of precious metals, minerals and real estate. Those banks permitted to operate with foreign currency tried to attract same for their equity capital. The equity capital containing foreign currency found itself growing with the decline of the ruble exchange rate. An instruction of the central bank on August 10, 1992 has changed this situation. According to it, paid-up equity capital should not be re-appraised in terms of foreign currency and must be shown in the balance at the ruble exchange rate for the date of signing the constituent contract or for another date specified by shareholders.

In accordance with this instruction, bank assets (excepting fixed assets) and liabilities should be revalued on the basis of the current ruble exchange rate set by the central bank (the equity capital remains without changes). The results of this reappraising are to be shown on the balance sheet account specifically designated for this purpose, "the Reappraising of Hard Currency Assets." Banks are allowed to show the exchange rate differentials in the balance accounts of income and expenses only once a year, at the end of the operations on December 31.

Nevertheless, the operations involving foreign currency are very attractive for banks. This is proved by the dynamics of the summary balance of commercial banks functioning on the territory of Russia. The hard currency current accounts of these banks grew from 2.6 billion rubles at the beginning of 1992 to 639.9 billion rubles on July 1, and amounted to 24.6% of all liabilities of commercial banks. The hard currency accounts are excluded from the reserve requirements of the central bank. Meanwhile, the share of foreign currency in commercial bank assets has grown from 0.5% in January to 27.6% in July.

Precious metals have not yet played a significant role, because the central bank preferred not to give licenses for operations with them to commercial banks.

Many large banks tried to diversify their activity to insure higher profitability of their operations. They have set up numerous trade houses, brokerage offices, investment institutions, insurance companies, consulting firms and advertising agencies under their control. Taking into consideration that the profit rate for brokerage operations was several times higher than that for banking operations, some commercial banks preferred not to take interest on their credits, but rather their share in the profit accrued from trade transactions.

Inflation influenced the interbank competition for the attraction of resources of big clients. It can be expected that with resources getting more expensive, the banks will mainly compete for the attraction of cheap resources (i.e., the balances of the current accounts of their clients). Banks will also compete for dealing with operations involving foreign currency.

5. The Process of Privatization in Russia

A.D. Radyguin
A.D. Krasnoselski

A. *The Establishment of Legal Framework*

Despite numerous political, administrative and methodological problems, Goskomimushestvo or GKI (the State Committee on State Property) managed to complete the elaboration of the concept of privatization by the beginning of summer 1992, which was reflected in a set of new documents published in June-August 1992.

Two fundamental laws actually dated back to June 1991: the Privatization of State and Municipal Enterprises Law and the Inscribed Privatization Accounts and Deposits Law. In December 1991, the Major Provisions of State and Municipal Enterprises Privatization Program for 1992 were decreed by President Yeltsin. In January 1992, seven obligatory acts were approved, including the Assessment of Assets Belonging to Enterprises, the Transformation of State Enterprises into Open (State) Companies and the Auctions and Tenders acts. Furthermore, other documents were approved in the period between winter and summer 1992, including, for instance, Yeltsin's decree "On the Sale of Land to Individuals and Juridical Persons when Privatizing State and Municipal Enterprises" (signed on March 25).

At the same time, most of the documents turned out to be temporary and declarative by their nature. There are two reasons for this. First, the nature of the Russian privatization model is controversial and at the same time a compromise. Because of this, monthly changes in tactics and strategy make the provisions obsolete very rapidly. Secondly, many of these acts were not concerned with the implementation procedures, or, on some key issues, referred to documents which had not yet been worked out. All this naturally has impeded the privatization process. Therefore, the stability and the clarity of obligatory acts are of fundamental importance.

In April 1992, GKI presented to the Supreme Soviet of Russia its version of the National Privatization Law. Because of heated debates, "On Changes and Amendments to the Privatization of State Enterprises Law" was not approved until June.

Though no fundamental amendments were actually adopted, the rejection of alternative proposals concerning expansion of incentives for the workers and the introduction of additional restrictions on foreign investors put forward by Russian communists and labor unions can be qualified a real success.

According to the Russian legislation, auctions and tenders are the basic methods of privatizing enterprises both under liquidation and those in operation. They can also be used in the sale of property. This, taken together with the ban on establishing closed (private) companies with state participants or assets as part of their initial capital, is aimed at limiting spontaneous privatization.

The National State and Municipal Enterprise Privatization Program for 1992 was approved by a resolution of the Supreme Soviet on June 11. Adopted after several delays, this program is a compromise between a "paid" model of privatization (for the active part of population) and its "free of charge" model (vouchers for all the people and incentives for the workers) on the one hand, and "a public privatization model for everybody" (GKI) and the property distribution among the employees (the communists and labor unions) on the other. According to the experts, this program provides investors, at least domestic ones, with rather acceptable conditions and terms, and on some issues even improves the "Major Provisions."

In comparison with the "Major Provisions" (auctions, commercial tenders, open [state] companies, the ban on redemption of leasing contracts and on bids tendered by only one buyer, the fixed system of incentives for the workers, etc.), "the assortment" of the possible methods of privatization is considerably diversified. For example, the program permits noncommercial investment tenders, and direct sale in the case of their failure. It also stipulates that the assets of enterprises which have already been liquidated and those being liquidated can be sold only at auctions. The main feature of this new concept of privatization is the formal expansion of incentives and opportunities for the workers, which were called unprecedented by Vice Premier Anatoly Chubais (who is also chairman of the GKI). But with the growth of worker access to management and control, this privatization procedure loses its "free of charge" nature.

Presidential decree N623 "On Measures to Support and Recover the State Enterprises Declared Bankrupt and to Employ Special Procedures Toward Them," dated June 14, 1992, has become the subject of heated debates. While this document makes the government market program complete, its effectiveness is in doubt. Insolvency and bankruptcy are not strictly defined by this decree. They can be applied to any state enterprise with a state share in its ownership capital of less than 50%. At the same time, the procedures may be prolonged for a period up to 2.5 years. The decree does offer a new method of privatization: carrying out of tenders on the sale of property of an enterprise declared bankrupt.

On June 30, 1992, the Supreme Soviet of Russia approved the draft law "On Insolvency (Bankruptcy) of the Enterprises." Although it is a positive step, the law's provisions will in all likelihood be mitigated by the predominance of state ownership, the producers' monopoly and the lack of necessary infrastructure (unpreparedness of the courts of arbitration).

On June 14, 1992, another presidential decree ratified the document defining the procedure of the sale of land under the privatization and expansion of state and municipal enterprises. This document is also applicable to the sale of land to individuals for their business activity. This document is of paramount importance, for it provides domestic and foreign entities and individuals the right to buy a piece of land after the privatization of an enterprise and to acquire additional pieces of land when carrying out production expansion. Nevertheless, the failure of the deputies to ratify private ownership of land, along with the contradictions between local legislative and executive powers and the traditional administrative practice of "determining" normative prices, make the legislation on privatization unworkable.

The compulsory character of transformation of a considerable number of large state enterprises into open companies (nearly 3,000 in 1992 and nearly 7,000 on the whole) is determined by at least two considerations:

- the issue of vouchers is considered by GKI as a major channel of the expansion of "the investment demand" on the part of population. In this sense, the transformation of a considerable number of enterprises into stock companies is necessary to ensure the adequate "investment supply"; and

- share ownership (even without the change of owners) can ensure the effective attraction of capital and its movements between economic sectors, given the scarcity of financing (i.e., profits, budget and bank credits, etc.).

According to some, the decree, can be regarded as a decisive step toward transfer of state enterprises to private capital (first of all, due to legalizing trust mechanisms which provide actual privatization without large expenditures on the part of private investors). Nevertheless, though extreme time pressure is caused by "adjusting" privatization to the voucher program, it does not make the dates more realistic.

According to the decree, corporatization had to be completed by October 1 (the deadline of handing in documents by the heads of enterprises), and state registration of new joint stock companies had to be done by November 1. Nevertheless, by September 1, only the norms for the first stage--that of establishing joint stock companies on the basis of state enterprises before privatization--were completely outlined. There still does not exist the key statute of stock-sale. The same is true about two more documents particularly important for the ideology of the decree: the trust statute and the long-promised set of documents on the participation of foreign investors in the privatization process.

GKI's aim to regulate strictly all the privatization procedures is undoubtedly of positive character, given spontaneous tendencies, the legal vacuum and conflicting local laws. But in addition (though it can be accounted for by large amount of work to be done within strict time boundaries), there are several negative features typical of the adopted documents; the inadequate quality of the documents themselves is self-evident: (for example, in the model regulations the allowed degree of deviation from the model is not clear; the procedures of changing the equity capital are not clear; initially the number of directors is limited to four formal members, making this body a nominal one instead of one that really represents the interests of proprietors, etc.). In addition, implementation documents following the decree appear only after with a considerable delay (as compared with the general dates of the decree implementation).

B. *Voucher Program*

The voucher program was adopted by the government on July 11. Privatization checks (vouchers) are federal securities with a limited (1 year) period of implementation, equal in value to 10,000 rubles, and are given to the bearer with the right to free sale (as distinct from the terms of the decree of July 3, 1992).

The program fosters the sale for vouchers of regional and federal property enterprises (according to Chubais--up to 40%-50% of state property). It also stipulates the possibility of voucher payment of up to 35% of value in the open sale of a privatized enterprise or purchase for vouchers of up to 35% of initial capital. Among other things, this means that all expenses of the program are taken by the federal budget, its share in the proceeds from privatization being 35%, with the remainder distributed among local budgets.

One of the key problems in the preparation of the voucher program was determining its nominal value as well as its real purchasing power. According to Chubais, GKI based its estimates on the real value of state enterprises and other property which could be sold for vouchers (35%, or approximated 1.4 trillion rubles in old balance prices). Vouchers can be used to buy property at prices based on the book value of assets according to the latest balance sheet estimation, which means the voucher's purchasing power will be higher than the equivalent sum of rubles at the 1992 rate, and the market price of the vouchers will be growing. At a meeting with administrative leaders and industry directors of the Amur region on September 1, Chubais claimed that in keeping with rising prices, the value of one voucher should be about 150,000-200,000 rubles.

Nevertheless, the quoting of vouchers, according to the Deputy Chairman of GKI, D. Vassilyev, is the main concern of this institution. It is believed that after a closed subscription all the shares left will be sold by auctions, giving priority to voucher payment over cash, which is why the real value of the voucher must be several times as high as the nominal value.

The agitation of GKI (especially under the conditions when it is practically impossible to predict the development of the situation) is not without grounds, and this is proved by the variety of opinions among independent experts: if *Commersant* (N. Kirichenko, M. Rogozhnikov) estimates the underlying value of each voucher in terms of privatized funds as only 333 rubles, then *Izvestia* (I. Karpenko) evaluates one voucher in relation to the enterprise fund worth "no less than $20,000."

One more essential problem is the influence of the voucher program on the arrangement of the participants in the privatization process. The incongruence between the location of funds and industrial capacities on the one hand, and population density on the other, leads to disproportions in voucher privatization. A fixed proportion of stock sale by the regional property funds for vouchers (35%) with the opportunities for localizing the financial markets puts the implementation of the socially vital voucher program of the government beyond the control (not in procedure, but in implementation) of the federal government, enhancing the dominant position of property funds in the privatization process.

Collusion among committees, property funds and commercial structures (in particular by establishing state bodies of investing companies) shifts the "burden" of privatization profits from the budget to the "friendly" commercial structures.

C. *Organizational Basis*

By the beginning of the summer, property committees had been established in 88 regions of Russia, with a total staff of about 10,200. In the majority of cases, it was to the local committees that GKI transferred the rights of territorial agencies (they were 91 in number), keeping for itself the function of appointing the chairman and dictating the local committee's budgets. In this way, according to some estimations, though the privatization process is actually shifting to the "provinces," GKI preserves control levers in personnel and finance policy. Its exclusive right to issue and interpret the normative acts within the bounds of its competence ends local law production.

In the interests of strengthening both the scientific-methodological and personnel bases of privatization, the Institute of Privatization Problems and the High School of Privatization and Enterprises were established under the auspices of Goskomimushestvo.

In order to "credit on favorable terms the citizens of Russia volunteering to take part in privatization," a commercial bank of privatization was established on government order with joint-stock capital of 300 million rubles (151 million from the federal and regional committees, 149 million from the property funds and other interested parties).

D. *The Dynamics of Privatization Process in General*

Besides rather productive legislative activity, one can observe the speeding-up of the process of "official" privatization. In January 1992, 1,430 privatization applications were registered; by August, there were more than 55,000 (Table 22).

The fiscal effect of privatization, although not a primary characteristic, can give, together with the dynamics of applications, a quantitative "snapshot" of the development of the privatization process. If in 1991 the value of privatized property was 2 billion rubles (from 500 industrial enterprises and 127 commercial and everyday service enterprises) and the budget profit was 200 million rubles, in January-August 1992 government budgets alone received 10.2 billion rubles, with the total value of privatized property of about 20 billion rubles. Dynamics viewed through 10-day periods show that in March the rate of privatization was 5-6 times as high as in January, while in August it was 10 times as high as in January.

In the first quarter of 1992, 5,023 applications were made; by August 1, there were 12,015 applications, although the actual rate of privatization "by fact" is much lower. To a great extent it is connected with an unstable normative privatization basis. Also, in almost all regions, the privatization process started with buying back leased assets; in the first quarter this type of privatization covered about 90%, in spring and summer 60%-70%. This can be accounted for by the fact that such enterprises have joined in the process of responsible ownership earlier than others, and, on the other hand, by a lower selling-price within the given type of privatization (the average selling-price of commercial and everyday services enterprises is as a rule 10 times lower when redeemed from lease than when sold by auction or on contest).

E. "Big" and "Small" Privatization

In this sphere the rate of privatization is the lowest. By August 1, only 1% of industrial enterprises had changed by type of ownership. In the first quarter of 1992, 59 enterprises were turned into open joint stock companies, but from January through June there were only 135, the greater part of which were in Karelia and the Arkhangelsk and Volgograd regions. No industrial enterprises were privatized in Daghestan, Kabardino-Balkaria, North Ossetia, Amur, or the Chelyabinsk and Kaliningrad regions.

According to the Vice Chairman of GKI, O. Kachanov, by fall about 400 big state industrial enterprises should be made private. Taking into account compulsory stock privatization, this number will grow up to 3,000 by the end of 1992. The factual dynamics of the process are less promising, however, because each big privatization project takes at least 5-6 months.

The process of privatization with regard to municipal property has been rapidly developing of late. The rate of privatization here is the highest (Table 23), though it is still lower than planned by the state program. By August, 7,600 retail shops (4.4%), 2,300 cafes and restaurants (1.7%), and 4,800 everyday services centers (3.8%) were made private.

The highest number of retail shops privatized was in Moscow (38% of all the city's shops) and the Sakhalin (18%) and Orel (19%) regions. In general, in the Volgo-Vyatka, Povolzhje, and Ural regions, out of 12,034 retail shops, 522 (4.3%) were sold, as were 121 cafes and restaurants out of 6,424 (1.9%), and 187 everyday service centers out of 4,492 (4.2%). No objects of "small" privatization have yet been sold in the Astrakhan region and Kalmykia, and the sale rate is very low in the Mordovia, Udmurtia, Ulyanov, Kirov, Kaliningrad, Tomsk, Moscow and Irkutsk regions. Although privatization is gradually becoming a commonplace phenomenon, the process of "small" privatization has not yet become irreversible.

From the point of view of the manner of privatization, sale by tender, in which case the owners commit themselves to certain conditions, predominates (40% of retail shops, 26% of cafes and restaurants, 47% of everyday services centers); next comes redemption from lease (29%, 41%, and 34%, respectively) and sale by auction (28%, 29%, and 11%).

F. *Privatization of Non-Completed Building Objects and Housing*

According to RF government enactment N59, Goskomstat conducted an accounting of non-completed buildings sold in the first half of the year. By July 1, 83 objects were sold for the sum of 500 million rubles, of which half belonged to municipal property, the same number belonged to oblasts, and only 3 to federal property.

Between January-February 1992, 548,000 flats became private, that is, 1.6% of the total number of flats potentially "privatizable." (The total floor-space of privatized flats is 27 million square meters, the average floor-space of a flat is 50 square meters.) Compared with the first half of 1991, these numbers grew roughly 11 times. In 1992, 765,400 flats will be privatized, with floor-space approximately 39.8 million square meters (including 403,800 flats privatized free of charge, with total floor-space of 21 million square meters).

According to official data, by August 1992 more than 400 privatizing agencies were established in the Russian Federation strictly for housing.

G. *Interaction of Privatization Bodies*

As privatization shifted from procedures to actual processes, the controversy between the property funds and the GKI began to grow, having its roots in the law of privatization. A government body, GKI has continued to assert its right to determine privatization procedure, attempting to limiting the functions of the parliamentary-controlled funds.

On the other hand, property funds have more and more claims to their own policy of privatization, especially as the funds are becoming the key figures in the course of actual privatization. They have tried to eliminate the GKI influence on the shareholding policy of privatized enterprises and on stock-sale tactics (speed, portion, location, the right to choose and enlist investing institutions, the handing over of the right of stock-sale by fund warrant, etc.). In the field of owning and operating stocks, the funds strive for monopolizing the terms of trust agreements--in place to preserve the rights of owners--and the very right of delegating authority when handing over the stocks of privatized enterprises into trust ownership.

Another aspect of the interaction of privatization bodies is the changing relationship of federal and regional privatization structures, especially as the very idea of federal property becomes blurred. The process of differentiating between different types of property is unconscionably slow. By the end of August, in only 8 out of 88 national-administrative and territorial subdivisions were property types differentiated. At the same time, local

67

authorities adopt unilateral resolutions on the acquisition of federal and state property. Such ambiguity in property differentiation leads to political instability.

Simultaneously, regional property funds get warrants from the federal fund to conduct privatization procedures with the shares of privatized federal objects. In those regions where GKI and the funds received exclusive rights from federal departments, practically all key decisions on federal property are adopted without consulting federal authorities. Formally the property is federal, but in reality Russian authorities do not control privatization instruments in these regions.

H. *Property Funds--Enterprises: Transformation of Spontaneous Privatization*

Spontaneous forms of privatization of the "nomenklatura-bureaucratic" type have adjusted themselves to new conditions, and taking on legitimate shape, have been transformed along two main lines (depending on the actual status quo between administration and privatization bodies in the regions on the one hand, and enterprises represented by their directors on the other). In the changing general policy of privatization, the regional funds aim not at effective sales but rather at gaining controlling interest over privatized enterprises.

Taking into account that the funds are dealing with local authorities and not the federal government (due to the mechanism of their formation), the local administrations and funds, employing privatization instruments, aim at controlling profit distribution and industrial production of privatized enterprises in local interests. Any countervailing pressure in which fund budgets are based on the effectiveness of their sale records appears to be insufficient. In those cases when the enterprise directors are a real force in the region, the funds and directors have come to agreements supporting directors' exclusive control over privatized enterprises.

I. _Amalgamations, Associations, Ministry Concerns and Corporations_

The president's decree on corporatization brought about new activity by the former governing superstructure in practically all branches. Depending the level of self-assertion, the claims of the given structures differ considerably: from mere transformation into joint stock enterprises by enterprise-founders (they take upon themselves service and coordination, but not administrative, functions) to the formation of holding companies with controlling interests in the key enterprises of branches.

Government bodies react differently to the activities of these structures due to the absence of unified policy towards vertical and horizontal integration on the basis of ownership. Different departments adopt different approaches to this issue. GKI and the antimonopoly committee, in accordance with their tasks, strive for greater structural disintegration in the process of privatization, doing away with artificial administrative links. Industrial ministries stand for preserving vertical integration in privatization mechanisms to maintain manageability and prevent industrial recession as a result of growing structural disintegration.

Compromise variations concerned with relegating stocks of enterprises allotted to property funds to the trust of state-controlled structures (decree on federal contract system) conflict with privatization instruments (decree on stock privatization, law of privatization). However, the issue of optimal trust management and its subject in a transition economy is by no means simple. If one follows strict privatization procedures assigned by GKI (by which only non-state structures can be subjects of trusts), this can lead to the lack of capable managers. One likely result will be the strengthening position of property funds. Therefore, the property funds system may turn into a super-ministry with branch divisions and subdivisions. Another possible scenario is to transfer real control over stocks left in state possession to the directors of privatized enterprises.

J. *Regional Specificity*

Notwithstanding the fact that all property committees started from equal positions (staff, premises and normative basis provision), the practical results of privatization are essentially different in different regions. The privatization rate is highest where senior administrators take pains with these issues. In particular, it is connected with the presence (or absence) of privatization income on the committees' accounts.

The majority of committees, nevertheless, do not require budget subsidies but become sources of budget revenue. The situation is worse in those GKI where their chairmen are not (against the legislation) deputy heads of local administration (e.g., the Udmurtia, Kabardino-Balkaria, Kalmykia, Chuvashia, Tuva, North Ossetia, Altaj, Kaliningrade and Moscow regions).

Actual privatization process in terms of regions is fastest in Central Russia and in industrial centers where the main objects liable to privatization are concentrated, such as the Perm, Sverdlovsk, Penza, Nizhny Novgorod, Volgograd, Belgorod, Kaluga and Krasnodar regions.

Administrative territories--traditional suppliers of raw materials or those on which objects of federal and departmental property are mainly located--have practically nothing but municipal assets (not large in stock). In these regions, the privatization process is hampered by the political opposition of both new and old structures (e.g., the Omsk and Saratov regions). In the Moscow region, according to property committee chairman V. Kleshnev, the very low privatization rate is accounted for by the absence of branch programs.

If the process of privatization in Nizhny Novgorod can be viewed as "ideal," then in the Vladimir region it is "average" and unsatisfactory in the Magadan region.

Thus, in the city of Nizhny Novgorod by August 1, more than 200 objects of small business were privatized (250 million rubles), while in the surrounding oblast 377 objects were privatized. 70%-80% of objects were sold by weekly auctions. The first auctions dealt with shops, currently everyday service centers are being auctioned, and soon so will wholesale trade and transport. Foreign investors have been allowed to take part in the auctions since October 1.

At a press conference on July 30, Chubais suggested that local authorities (municipalities) should use the Nizhny Novgorod model as the standard of mass small privatization. The specific qualities of this model were the "20 principles" worked out with the help of Goskomimushestvo and International Finance Corporation experts. Among other things, priority is given to the most objective auction method; there is a policy against one-piece ownership; there are stimuli for investments into privatized enterprises modernization by means of bringing down rent payment in proportion to investments made;

71

before privatization, state enterprises are abolished as such and their debts are transferred to the municipality; and there are no obligations on preserving the former staff.

In the Vladimir region, 215 enterprises (including 28 industrial enterprises of regional importance) were privatized with proceeds of 300 million rubles by July 20; in the Magadan region, however, by the beginning of July none had been privatized. According to the leaders of the local property committee, it is due to a higher (as compared with central areas) value of industrial funds (by a factor of 3.5), remoteness from the center, high transport expenses, and the transient character of population.

In Sankt-Petersburg during the summer (by July 23), 4 open auctions and 5 closed contests were held; as a result, 66 objects were sold with a great price range, generating proceeds of 20 million rubles. Everyday services centers, shops and industrial sites, non-completed buildings, land lots, dwelling houses, and flats--a total of 4,000 objects--were auctioned off.

Moscow's specificity is conditioned by special authority in privatization sphere which was allotted to the Moscow government by a special presidential decree. Beside actual mass transfer of small privatization objects to corresponding staff, from April to June 26 non-completed buildings were sold for 150 million rubles. As a result of an open contest held by Moscow GKI, the right to sell these objects was gained by eight firms. At the same time this sphere of privatization in Moscow remains rather doubtful from a legal point of view, as the relations between the government and the Moscow soviet remain unclear; the same concerns the provision of property rights to the customer (are they given by Moskomimushestvo or the fund?). Potential customers at the moment have no rights to lease land or to ownership, and only the right "to complete the construction of a bought object by December 31, 1992."

The enactment of Moscow government "On the common procedure of estimation and management of premises in Moscow" came into effect on September 1. According to the experts, the established procedure of conducting auctions and contests is not drastically different from common practice.

6. Foreign Investments in the Russian Federation

S.N. Lavrov
I.V. Makarov
I.S. Mukhamedshin
S.V. Prikhotko
V.V. Ranenko

In the first six months of 1992, the inflow of direct foreign investment in the economy of the Russian Federation decreased considerably compared with the same periods in 1991 and 1990. But closer look shows that the number of the Russian-foreign ventures under registration is not decreasing as obviously as the *volume* of investments.

About 400 enterprises with foreign investments (EFI) were registered during the six months of this year, including 240 in the second quarter of the year; the total volume of coordinated foreign investment in registered enterprises is about 7.5 billion rubles, with more than 5 billion rubles of that coming in the second quarter. This equals approximately US$50 million.

The greatest number of EFI were organized with participation of firms from Germany (40 units) and the US (36 units). American and German investors remain the leaders in both the number of EFI registered in Russia and in the sum of coordinated investments. The registration of enterprises with participation of partners from Finland has practically ceased, but in previous years Finnish investors were among the leaders (to a great extent, this is connected with the traditional interest of Finnish businessmen in investments in the economy of Estonia, Latvia and Lithuania). The decrease in the interest of Finnish firms, as well as of firms from Great Britain, Austria and some other countries, in investing in the Russian economy reflects the change for the worse in the investment climate in the Russian Federation.

The notable phenomenon in the current process of the registration of EFI in the first six months is the growth of the number of the enterprises organized with participation of partners from China (17 enterprises), Poland (15), Bulgaria (15), Hungary and other countries with economies in transition from centralized planning to the market. One can forecast the further growth of such investments. Production of the firms of these countries finds exploitable demand in the Russian market sooner than in the markets of Western countries. The same refers to the technologies and financial resources of China, which is becoming a notable exporter of capital. East European countries see in the organization of joint ventures (JV) on the territory of Russia the means to the restoration and strengthening of cooperative and trade links, which constituted the basis for their previous external economic turnover. If Russian enterprises take into account these peculiarities in practice, they can attract investments from these countries on more favorable terms.

One should note the increasing activity of businessmen from the countries of the Middle East. In the first six months of 1992, more than 20 joint ventures were registered with participation of firms from Syria, Lebanon, Israel and other countries of this region.

In addition, there are first investments from those former Soviet republics which did not enter the ruble economic space. About 10 joint ventures with enterprises from these countries were organized in January-June.

The number of enterprises which fully belong to foreign investors is increasing (22 enterprises were registered in the first quarter of this year, 45 in the second quarter). It is significant that nearly a third of them were organized by American investors and are oriented to consulting and other business services to clients from the US and other Western countries.

The structure of direct foreign investment in the first six months confirms the trend of investing primarily in small enterprises organized for trade and intermediary operations, rendering business services to Russian and foreign businessmen, in the consumer goods trade, and for rendering services to people. Significant spheres for the investment of foreign capital are the lumber industry (as a rule, with the export of half-finished products as repayment for delivered equipment), residential construction (especially for well-off purchasers), and recycling of post-consumer waste.

More than 50% of the aggregate investment in the first six months was planned as contributions to the start-up capital of 10-15 joint ventures; in the second quarter, however, 95% of foreign investments went to 36 new joint ventures, which was only 15% of those registered in the quarter. The characteristic tendency is the increase in the average portion of foreign investments in the founding capitals of joint ventures (47% in the quarter), by which it is possible for foreign investors to receive very high returns in rubles for their small currency investments in the start-up funds of joint ventures by virtue of the decreasing exchange rate of the ruble to the hard currency.

Thus, the registration of EFI in Russia in the first six months of this year confirms the fact that the inflow of foreign investments in the economy of the Russian Federation is mainly stimulated by the desire of investors to organize their presence on the market of the RF and other countries of the CIS in the hope for current easy profits, including those of the export of raw materials and semi-finished products, export-import operations under the unstable price formation, and rendering services to the major investors for hard currency.

Industrial and economic activity of EFI is very dynamic (Table 24).

In the first six months of 1992, EFI accounted for 4.5% of all Russian exports and 2.4% of all Russian imports.

The results of the financial-economic activity of enterprises with foreign investments show that even despite the decrease in the production in the country and the general turn to the worse in the investment and economic climate, the productivity of labor and return on the funds of these enterprises are increasing and are considerably higher than the same indices for state enterprises. EFI still reinvest a considerable share of their profits in development, technical reequipment, and shifting to new kinds of activity.

The increase in the number of EFI and the expansion of the scope of their activity strengthen the market sector of the Russian economy, and introduce an element of international business culture. These enterprises are constantly increasing the volume and widening the range of production and services offered to the market. They promote the links of the Russian economy to the world. Moreover, foreign private investment in the enterprise on the territory of Russia is not an additional burden on the state budget, as the credits of the international financial organizations are. From this point of view, more intensive efforts to attract foreign private investment are cost-effective for reforming the Russian economy. The encouragement of foreign investments by the grant of guarantees and privileges and by assistance in "match making" between state property and foreign investors should be an important element in the state's long-term economic policy. As world practice shows, the mere presence in receiving countries (e.g., China, Mexico) of a potentially large home market, natural resources, and a cheap labor force do not of themselves ensure considerable foreign investment. Only the formation of an attractive investment climate with an effective legal system, provision of guarantees (of adherence to the law, among other things), and economic mechanisms and public consciousness suitable for enterprise development will ensure the confidence of foreign investors and the subsequent inflow of capital.

Quite a number of government actions opening new possibilities for foreign investments were taken in the second quarter of this year:

- a whole series of normative documents on the privatization of state and municipal property;

- the decision of the Russian central bank on the establishment of one and the same exchange rate of the ruble to foreign currencies in both current and capital operations;

- the decree of President Yeltsin "on measures for the development of free economic zones"; and

- the law "on currency regulation and currency control."

The possibility of the purchase of property in the course of privatization in the target countries, as the experience of, for example, Hungary, China and Czechoslovakia shows, is a serious incentive for attracting direct foreign investment. It could be especially strong in Russia, with its considerable but non-effective capital assets (the official [account] value of which is very often scanty, and of which market value is not determined, since there are no convincing methods and practice for forecasting profitability of the enterprises under privatization, and there is no market for the securities by which the shares of these enterprises could find "their price").

Documents now in force on the privatization of state and municipal enterprises encourage the participation of foreign investors in the privatization of commercial enterprises, public catering, consumer services, small industrial enterprises, building, motor transport (although exclusively by the decision of local Councils of People's Deputies), enterprises of the fuel and energy complex, and enterprises concerned with the extraction and processing of precious and semi-precious stones, metals and radioactive and rare-earth elements (only by the decision of the government of the RF or republics.

The program of privatization of state and municipal enterprises in the Russian Federation for 1992 dictates serious changes in procedures for attracting and using foreign investment in organizing joint ventures with the participation of Russian state and municipal founders. Firstly, property invested as capital in joint ventures by state (municipal) enterprises is recognized as state (municipal) property. Because the program decrees that "such an investment of property can be permitted only by the corresponding committees on the control of property," the first stage of privatization of state and municipal enterprises is practically devoid of the right to decide freely to attract foreign (and, by the way, Russian) investment. At the second stage of privatization (after the organization of open joint-stock companies), the participation of foreign (and Russian) investors in the purchase of shares of privatized enterprises is determined by the actions of competitive commissions. These commissions are organized by the property funds for carrying out lotteries and auctions (timing, terms, minimum pricing, etc.). In this case, the enterprise, its managers and work force are virtually denied the possibility of choosing an investor-purchaser of shares, with whom they will have to run the privatized enterprise.

The property funds have the right to decide on assigning the property of the enterprises under privatization to the start-up funds of other enterprises, including joint ventures with foreign investments; they also may have the right of veto on decisions to change the organization-legal form of the enterprise under privatization. Because of this, attracting foreign investment for the reequipment and development of the majority of current state- and municipal-owned enterprises may temporarily be possible only in the form of purchase of the shares of open joint-stock companies, which would hardly be acceptable for many investors, since the open joint-stock company has to publish its records, has relatively weak management by virtue of the great number of the holders of ordinary shares, and one of the stock-holders--the property fund--may reserve the right of veto on some key issues of the activity of the company.

It is obvious that some aspects of privatization regulation in Russia require urgent correction, especially because participation of foreign investors in privatization, which is critical, is not treated clearly enough in these documents. For example, if a foreign investor is the only participant in the auction sale of state enterprises or their shares, then the relevant property funds will evaluate the property according to methods approved by the State Property Committee. It would be reasonable to suggest that these methods will be more "firm" than in the case of the participation of Russian investors, which would belie the guarantee that terms of foreign investment and the activity of foreign investors "cannot be less favorable than the regime for the property, property rights and investment activity of the juridical persons and citizens of the RF" (Article 6 of the Law on Foreign Investments in the RF).

The documents adopted in June do not contain any statement which would stimulate the participation of foreign investors in privatization of unprofitable state enterprises, enterprises with low profitability, or the purchase of unfinished or mothballed objects of state and municipal property. Unfortunately, these peculiarities of the legal basis for privatization limit the attractiveness for foreign investors of that considerable part of the economic potential of Russia which now consisting of state and municipal property, worsening the investment climate in Russia.

It is obvious that in the process of privatization there will be problems connected with the implementation of the interests of the Russian citizens working at joint ventures which include state property as a major asset. The investments of the state (municipal) enterprises under privatization in the capital of joint ventures are included in the evaluation of the property of these enterprises, become a part of the share capital of new open joint-stock companies, and are privatized by the collective ownership of state enterprises (on favorable conditions) and also by their managers and purchasers of the shares of the property funds. The staff of joint ventures, by whose efforts in deploying the state property as an asset the joint venture brings profit, cannot claim the privileged purchase of the part of the state property with which they are immediately dealing.

This, from our point of view, does not correspond to one of the central ideas of privatization--favorable terms for the acquisition of property by those citizens who participate directly in the process of production. It seems to be reasonable to issue a special explanation on behalf of the State Committee of Property on granting privileges in privatization for the citizens working at those commercial enterprises which include state property as an asset or determinant of ownership. One of the possible ways of solving this problem is the following: if state property is included in the value or the property of the state enterprise which is under privatization and, at the same time, the enterprise is a founder of a joint venture, then the Russian workers of the joint venture may become members of the working collective ownership of the enterprise and they can get shares according to the formula chosen. Another variant would be that the property fund temporarily possessing shares of the enterprises under privatization lets a part of these shares on favorable terms to the workers of the joint venture.

The decision to use for discount or currency operations the single exchange value of the ruble to foreign currencies, confirmed by the currency markets for a particular date, presents new possible solutions to the problem of the currency self-repayment of enterprises with foreign investments. The guaranteed opportunity for sale and purchase of hard currency for rubles on the currency market will, if maintained for a sufficient period of time, lead to a natural increase in the confidence to the investment climate in Russia.

The declining exchange rate of the ruble to foreign currencies, the rise in prices, and other inflation manifestations require a change in some provisions of the legislation, including those concerned with foreign investments. For example, it is necessary to change Article 16 of the law "On foreign investments in the RF" about the need to receive special permission of the Cabinet of Ministers for the registration of enterprises which exceed 100 million rubles in terms of foreign investment volume. Given the present exchange value of the ruble (one can hardly forecast the increase in the "price" of the ruble in hard currency in the near future), such permission should be given to enterprises with foreign investments equivalent to roughly US$650,000-$700,000. The same refers to the requirement of the State Committee on Antimonopoly Legislation to coordinate with it the registration of enterprises with the funding capital of more than 50 million rubles (or, at the present time, $350,000). These enterprises can hardly be regarded as potential monopolists.

In the first six months of the year, other statutes immediately concerned with foreign investment and improving the investment climate in Russia were adopted:

- Decree of the President of the RF N 631 ("On the sale of land lots to citizens and juridical persons during the privatization of state and municipal enterprises"), which allots to the purchasers of the enterprises under privatization, including foreign investors, the right to purchase property on corresponding lots, including the lots necessary for the development and reconstruction of these enterprises;

- Resolution of the Supreme Soviet N 3257-1 ("On the introduction of changes in the Resolution of the Supreme Soviet of the RF on Taxation"), which returned to enterprises with foreign investments in the sphere of material production registered before January 1, 1992 the abatement from the tax on profit for 2 years (in the long-term economic implementation--for 3 years);

- The law "On Security," which legalizes the right of foreign investors, banks, other juridical and physical persons to mortgage and to take as mortgages the property invested on the territory of the RF or accumulated on the basis of these investments; and

- The law "On the introduction of changes and additions in the taxation system of Russia," which returned tax abatement to enterprises on any form of property used for the "technical re-equipment of the process of production in all spheres of national economy," and not only in the oil, coal and medical industries and in the production of foodstuffs.

It should be noted that though these decisions of the Supreme Soviet and the President return the conditions on the activity of enterprises with foreign investments to the level of the second six months of 1991, on the whole these conditions have become worse and, what is more important, foreign investors cannot be sure of the stability of the present investment climate.

We may also note that some of the recent decrees of the President are in contradiction with the law "On foreign investments." Thus, Decree N629 "On the partial changes in the order of the obligatory sale of the part of the currency receipts and collection of the export duties" obliges enterprises, including enterprises with foreign investments, to sell half of their currency receipts at currency auction, but the law leaves all the currency receipts at the disposal of enterprises. Decree N630 "On the temporary import customs-tariff in the RF" practically abrogates the emancipation from customs duties of EFI importing goods necessary for the process of production.

Distrust of the investment climate in Russia is conditioned not only by the abrupt changes in the taxation legislation, but by other factors which are more important for foreign investors:

- political instability and the growing tension of social conflicts in Russia and some other countries of the CIS;

- the weakness of contract practice in economic relations;

- the abrupt lowering of the solvency of purchasers on the domestic production and consumer markets; and

- bureaucratic complication and corruption.

Some of these factors influence the position of different investors in different ways. According to the central interests they pursue in the course of investment, these investors can be subdivided into four groups.

1. Investors whose aim is the use of the natural resources of Russia, return on investments, and increase in profitability through export of resources: These are big firms with considerable capital for the implementation of concession contracts or agreements on prospecting and the extraction of minerals. Such agreements are achieved, as a rule, on the basis of talks with the state organs and on terms, which are discussed separately. The most important factors for these investors are political and social stability in the host country, clear-cut limits of authority and division of power between administrative bodies at all levels as far as the decisions on the use of the territory are concerned, and the presence in the country of transport and energy infrastructure. The general state of economy, weakness of domestic demand, nonconvertability of the local currency and even the bureaucratic obstacles have less influence on their decisions. At present in Russia there is a favorable climate for such investors, because of the existence of the unused reserves of oil, gas and other natural resources, and because the state has an urgent need for hard currency.

2. Investors whose aim is the production on Russian territory of industrial and consumer goods for the home market with the use of local basic funds (mainly passively), raw materials, materials, labor power, and infrastructure. It is through these investments that the economy of the country is enriched with foreign technological and organizational experience. The most important among them are the enterprises supplying Russian enterprises with equipment, materials and other production components, which reduces import dependency and consequently decreases the tension in exports. The majority of the investors in these ventures can be referred to as the "small" or middle class. The ventures are organized, as a rule, on common, unsophisticated terms, which is why they depend on

judicial and practical protection of their property, on the guarantees of contract relations in economic practice, on the possibility of exchanging their receipts from rubles to hard currency, on the peculiarities of the customs regime, and on the "liberal" exercise of bureaucratic procedures. At present the investment climate in Russia is the most complex for this group of enterprises with foreign investments. Officially, they can receive their receipts only in rubles. Often breaches of delivery and of the terms of payments are not compensated, which puts these enterprises in a very difficult position. Scant information about domestic commodity producers, the complexity involved in the purchase and lease of premises and other property, and the tyranny of bureaucracy are also real problems for these enterprises. Abrogation of tax privileges in the first years of profitable activity and high taxes (including the tax on the reinvested profit--except investments in technical reequipment, which are hardly essential for joint ventures in the first years of their existence) both show the unwillingness of the state to stimulate productive direct investment, and investors understand it as a deliberate element of the economic policy of Russia. In this way, Russia differs unfavorably from other countries of the CIS. From our point of view, the investors of this group, especially when they organize the production of the goods which are usually imported, should be granted serious privileges in taxation, encouraged to reinvest profits, guaranteed the integrity of the juridical terms of activity, and facilitated access to state property under privatization.

3. Investors whose main aim is importing foreign consumer goods and ready-made production goods to Russia, and purchasing of raw materials and semi-finished products for export.

4. Firms investing their capital in the production of goods and services for major investors, mainly from the first group, and also for foreign judicial persons (corporations) who organize building, installing and other works in Russia. We think that the investors of the third and fourth groups can be granted the terms of activity common for all businessmen in the country.

One of the central aims of attracting foreign investments is increasing the effectiveness of Russia's technological exchange with other countries. The main tendencies in the spread of technology through direct foreign investments in the Russian economy, revealed in the first quarter of this year, are still dominant, connected first of all with the policy of stabilizing the economy. Though all over the world business undertakings are considered to be an optimal way of attracting modern technology, in the Russian economy there is no considerable inflow of the newest foreign technologies, and foreign investors only reluctantly deliver the newest technologies to joint ventures with Russian businessmen. They prefer to invest small means in those sectors where it is possible either to bring the results of experiments, scientific research and design works into commercial use in Russia, or to transfer Russian intellectual products to concrete high technologies, with further export of them to the West. From these sectors, one can single out the conversion productions of the military industrial complex, laser welding and surface thermo-strengthening of metals, milling and drilling of superfirm materials, ceramics, treatment of uncut diamonds, and artistic treatment of plastics, wood and fabrics. For example, foreign businessmen invest in the specialists who prepare software products for sale to Western firms which produce computer systems. One of the recent examples is the organization of the private corporation

"Russian-American Science" in Delaware by the Russian Academy of Sciences (RAN) and two American firms. The corporation was organized for promoting RAN programs on the American market.

Such a position of foreign investors can be explained by several reasons:

1. Up to now, there has been no clearly formulated state policy regulating the inflow of foreign technologies and the outflow of Russian technologies through foreign investments.

2. Market factors are not strong enough to influence seriously the conduct of Russian businessmen in the field of introduction of newest technologies.

3. The Russian home market, despite its potential as a whole, is not ready for technologies of a sufficiently high level. Obsolete equipment and the absence of the necessary materials and spare parts make the problem of the assimilation of new technologies (not only imported ones) a difficult task.

4. There are still export control limitations in the legislation of some Western countries on the transmission of the newest technologies to the former socialist countries by COCOM members.

Finally, demand by Russian enterprises might not be high because of the insolvency crisis and the absence of the sufficient currency means. Perhaps the only stimulus for the continuation of the research projects in Russia, for the introduction of projects into production, was the demand of the world markets and agreements on international scientific-technical cooperation with foreign partners.

Among the most urgent needs, it is possible to single out the following:

1. The formulation, as quickly as possible, of a technological policy for Russia, the aims and means of which were previously formulated in the "Program on the Intensification of Economic Reforms" in coordination with other states of the CIS.

2. State support for the process of formation of the valuable institutions of the technology market. Only such institutions will be able to create a "working" effective economy and competitive environment.

3. The problem of preservation of domestic scientific and technical potential from the scattering of specialists, including "brain drain," is vital and great.

4. The regulation and guarantees of the protection of intellectual property, which will have a decisive impact on production in the process of scientific and technical cooperation with foreign partners.

It should be noted that at present the inflow of private foreign capital in the economy of Russia is poorly stimulated by the development of new--as compared with traditional--joint business forms of attracting foreign investment. In the "free economic zones" (the FEZ, such as the Altai Territory, the Jewish Autonomous Region, and others), it is practically impossible to create an acceptable investment environment, and particularly infrastructure, because of local and central budget financial means. In other FEZ (e.g., Nahodka, Viborg), the process is handicapped by the lack of experience in the organization of such "enclaves" and by the presence of the state enterprises which are not subordinate to the administration of the zones and cannot be included in the programs of the development and the systems of economic relations which are now being elaborated by the administration. Apparently, FEZ will work more actively if, in the course of the implementation of the decree of the President on the measures of their development, both general and specific regulations are revised. It will ensure a greater concentration of power by the administrative committees of the FEZ, accelerate privatization of state and municipal property on their territories, and put their budgets in order.

APPENDIX A

TABLES

Table 1
The Rate of Decrease of National Income and Production in Industry
(% to 1991, comparable prices)

Period	National Income	Industrial Production
January	15	15.1
January-February	15	13.5
January-March	14	13
January-April	14	12.7
January-May	17	13.2
January-June	18	13.5
January-July	18	14.8

Table 2
The Structure of Industrial Production for January-July

	Structure of Production of January-July 1991	Structure of Production of January-July 1992
Industry as a whole	100	100
Electric power production	4.6	5.7
Fuel industry	8.6	13.0
Ferrous metallurgy	5.2	9.8
Non-Ferrous metallurgy	6.6	9.4
Chemical and oil industry	7.8	9.9
Machine building and metal processing	25.0	22.0
Timber industry and wood processing industry	5.9	5.5
Building materal industry	3.2	2.7
Food industry	10.9	9.1
Light industry	15.5	9.6

Table 3
Dynamics of Export and Import Transactions ($ Billion)

	Export	Import	Balance	Turnover
January	2.2	2.2	0	4.4
January-February	6.0	8.0	-2	14.0
January-March	7.0	9.2	-2.2	16.2
January-April	10.7	11.4	-0.7	22.1
January-May	12.4	12.4	0	24.8
January-June	15.4	14.9	+0.5	30.3
January-July	18.4	19.1	-0.7	37.5

Table 4
The Main Indices of Russian Foreign Trade in the Summre of 1992*

	Export	Import	Balance
June			
$ Billion	3.0	2.5	+0.5
%, 1992/1991	65.0	65.0	
July			
$ Billion	3.0	4.2	-1.2
%, 1992/1991	88.0	108.0	

* Callculated by the Russian Federation State Statistics Committee

Table 5
Exports of the Main Kinds of Power Resources in June and July of 1992

Kind of Resources	June	July	June 1991 %	July 1991 %
Black coal (thousands of tons)	2400	1200	118.6	77.7
Crude oil (thousands of tons)	4424	3876	95.5	96.5
Natural gas	6.6	7.3	101.7	105.8

Table 6
Imports of the Main Kinds of Foodstuffs in the Summer of 1992

Kinds of Goods	1992		1991/1992 %		
	June	July	Jan./May	Jan./June	Jan./July
Corn (thousands of tons)	2045	1755	167	152	147
Meat (thousands of tons)	23.3	88.7	64	58	72
Potatoes (thousands of tons)	0.2254	58	45	48	N/A
Citric Fruit (thousands of tons)	0.130	23	21	N/A	N/A
Coffee	N/A	0.7	61	47	43

Table 7
Dynamics of income and expenses of the population in the Russian Federation
(1991-1992, Billion Rubles)

	Income	Expense	Imbalance Between Income and Expenses %
1991			
1st quarter	114.3	82.1	28
2nd quarter	143.3	106.3	26
3rd quarter	191.9	132.5	31
4th quarter	283.4	189.3	33
1992			
1st quarter	519.2	358.4	31
2nd quarter	919.6	586.5	33
July	510.9	258.8	49

Table 8
Commodity Turnover and Its Increase (Decrease) Rates
(In January-June of 1992, in January Prices)

	Turnover billions rubles	Increases in %, as compared with previous month	% to corresp. of 1991
January	74.2	---	37
February	89.9	+21	50
March	97.1	+7.9	50
April	94.8	-2.4	82
May	90.9	-4.1	67
June	95.2	+4.7	66

Table 9
Change of Combined Index for Consumer Prices

Period	% as compared with previous month	as compared with corresp. period of 1991
January	345	8.5 times
February	138	11.1 times
March	130	13.6 times
April	122	10.1 times
May	112	11.0 times
June	117	12.7 times

Table 10
Cost Change of Consumer Basket

	(% as compared with December 1991)
December 91	100
January 92	782
February 92	838
March 92	923
April 92	1090
May 92	1207
June 92	1333
July 92'	1387

Table 11
Consumer Expenses in the Families of Workers and Employees
(% of the total in May and June of 1992)

	May 1992	June 1992
Commodity expenses, total	100	100
Foodstuffs	43.6	43.4
Non-foodstuffs	41.3	42.5
Alcohol drinks	3.8	3.2
Services payments	11.3	10.9

Table 12
Russia's State Budget Structure by Levels of Administration, Realizing Its Implementation.

	1990			1991*			1992 (project)**		
	bln rbl	% of sum	% of VAT	bln rbl	% of sum	% of VAT	bln rbl	% of sum	% of VAT
State budget receipts total:	127.5	100	21.3	410.7	100	32.6	6325.8	100	40.8
Including:									
of federal budget	69.9	54.8	11.7	154.5	37.6	12.3	2358	37.3	15.2
of local budgets	57.6	45.2	9.6	144.9	35.3	11.5	1480	23.4	9.5
State budget expenditures total:	127.6	100	21.2	483.2	100	38.3	7056	100	45.5
including:									
of federal budget	69.9	54.8	11.7	235.8	48.8	18.7	3064	43.4	19.8
of local budget	57.7	45.2	9.6	172.5	35.7	13.7	1509	21.4	9.7

* In 1991 Stabilization Fund and Pension Fund are included into Russia's consolidated budget. Financing of agricultural products price difference, provided at the expense of the Central bank credit resources, is included into expenditures.

** In 1992 non-budget funds (623 bln. rbl.) and Pension Fund (1385,4 bln.rbl.), and also foreign economic activity income (479.5 bln. rbl.) are totally included into the Russia's consolidated budget income. Non-budget funds (2008.4 bln.rbl.) and foreign economic activity expenses (1569 bln. rbl.) are included into expenditures.

Source: Ministry of Finance, Statistics State Committee of Russia; authors' calculations.

Table 13
State Earning Reconstruction in the First Quarter, First Half-Year and 1992 (bln. rbl.)

	January-March	January-June	1992
Consolidated Budget Earnings	364.2	1040.3	4317.4***
Pension Fund Earnings	105.2	286**	1385.4
Traffic Fund Earnings	4.9	25.6	180.0
Employment Fund Earnings	2.1	4.9	38.4
Other Non-Budget Funds (R&D and conversion finance regulation)	---	---	404.6
Earnings of Republican Hard Currency Reserves at the Expense of Currency Purchase at the Exceed Exchange Rate of the Ruble*	38.5	93.5	192.5
TOTAL	514.9	1450.3	6518.3
GNP Percentage Total	38.3	36.2	42.1

* The estimate is given on the export data over the first quarter - $7 bln.rbl.; first half -$16.8 bln.rbl. The average sales were 10% of the hard currency including privileges with exchange rate 55 rbl/USD. During the second half the market rouble exchange rate was taken for hard currency purchases, so only the first half of 1992 was taken into account in estimating the earnings above.

** The estimate is given on the data of earnings over the first quarter, the dynamics of households' incomes over the first half of 1992.

*** The budget Earnings of 3837 bln.rbl. plus returns of foreign economic activity valued at 479.5 bln. rbl. plus the export tariff - 419.5 bln. rbl.

Sources: Russian Federation Ministry of Finance, the Center of Market Studies and Forecast under Economic Department of Russia; authors' calculations.

Table 14
Russian Federation Budget Execution on Income Items (monthly) over 1992.

	Revenues (bln. rbl.)						
	Jan.	Feb.	March	April	May	June	July
1. Excise tax & Turnovers tax	6.4** 1.8	7.6 1.8	9.0 1.6	8.1 1.1	9.2 1.1	11.0 1.0	9.7 1.0
2. Income tax	27.3 7.7	37.0 7.3	38.7 6.9	116.5 15.2	98.4 11.7	74.4 7.1	167.3 17.6
3. Property tax	---	---	---	1.5	1.6	0.8	5.7
4. Deducts to cover mining search cost	0.6 0.2	0.9 0.2	1.2 0.2	0.8 0.1	0.5 0.1	2.6 0.3	4.0 0.4
5. Value added tax & tax on sales	16.4 4.7	37.3 8.7	52.8 9.4	63.5 8.3	51.8 6.1	77.0 6.3	116.4 12.3
6. Rent payments	0.03	0.2	0.4	0.1	0.01	0.2	0.4
7. Income tax on cooperative & public organizations	1.7 0.5	1.4 0.3	1.2 0.2	3.2 0.4	1.5 0.2	0.2 0.02	-**
8. Personal taxes	7.8 2.2	9.5 2.2	15.1 2.7	17.7 2.3	19.0 2.2	24.5 2.3	28.8 3.0
9. Foreign trade earnings	1.1 0.3	4.2 1.0	4.8 0.9	29.5 3.3	8.6 1.0	13.6 1.3	18.0 1.9
10. Forestry earnings	0.1	0.5	0.7	0.5	0.2	0.7	1.0
11. State duty, local taxes	0.2	0.2	0.3	0.4	0.3	0.6	0.4
12. Charge for water	0.03	0.05	0.04	0.05	0.07	0.2	0.3
13. Charge for land	0.06	0.08	0.13	0.12	0.12	0.29	1.0
14. Charge for natural resources on precious metals	1.5 0.4	2.3 0.5	2.2 0.4	2.5 0.3	2.0 0.2	3.6 0.3	5.2 0.5
15. Total tax receipts	63.3 17.9	96.3 22.6	126.6 22.4	244.5 31.9	193.3 22.9	209.7 19.9	358.3 37.7
16. Other revenues	13.9	21.1	28.0	19.5	17.4	6.8	16.1
17. Total revenue	77.2	117.4	154.6	264.0	210.7	216.5	374.4
18. For reference: Gross national product (GNP)***	353	427	546	765	843	1054	950 ****

*   For large items share in GNP is given in the denominator.

**   From July 1992 is included in the income tax.

***   Data from the Economic Situation and Forecast Center of Russia's Ministry of Finance.

**** Preliminary data.

Source: Russia's ministry of Finance, State Tax Service data; calculations.

Table 15
Budget Receipts of Separate Types of Taxes by Accumulating Total For Seven Months of 1992 (% of GNP)

	Jan.	Feb.	March	April	May	June	July
1. Excise duty & tax on turnover	1.8	1.8	1.7	1.5	1.4	1.3	1.2
2. Income tax	7.7	7.6	7.3	10.2	10.6	9.7	11.2
3. VAT & tax on sales	4.7	6.9	7.9	8.1	7.5	7.5	8.4
4. Personal taxes	2.2	2.2	2.4	2.4	2.3	2.3	2.5
5. Total tax receipts	17.9	20.5	21.3	25.2	24.5	23.3	26.1

Source: See Table 14.

Table 16
National Economy Profit Dynamics by Months, 1992 (bln. rbl.)

	1991		1992					
	Nov.	Dec.	Jan.	Feb.	Mar.	April	May	June
On National economy (bln. rbl.)	24.9	52.3	95.4	175.2	298.6	210.5	199.3	378.5
In % to preceding month	---	210	182	184	170	-29	-5	190
Including industry (bln. rbl.)	21.3	34.3	84.8	151	246	184.9	165.4	257.5
In % to preceding month	---	161	247	178	163	-25	-10	156

Source: Russia's State Statistics Committee

Table 17
The Sources and Allocation of the Monetary Base from the Beginning of 1992: The Ratio to the Total Sum/the Ration to GNP of the previous year in annual terms. (%%)

	By the Beginning of 1992	By the Beginning of Second Quarter of 1992	By the Beginning of Second Part of 1992
Central bank credits to the government	65.5/30.1	48.5/7.0	41.4/8.8
Loans to commercial banks	29.0/13.3	41.8/6.0	35.5/7.6
Interstate payments	---	5.2/0.8	18.3/3.9
Foreign currency & precious metals	0.01/0.004	1.3/0.2	2.5/0.5
Commercial banks' reserves	50.0/16/7	48.4/4.5	60.3/8.7
Cash in circulation	49.1/16.7	51.6/4.7	39.6/5.7

Table 18
The Monetary Base Increase From the Beginning of 1992: Rates and Structure by Sources. (%%)

	Increase Rate					Structure	
	Monthly average first quarter	April	May	June	July	1st quarter	2nd quarter
Credits to the government	6.3	19.5	4.0	51.1	---	21.3	35.4
Loans	32.8	22.2	19.9	27.9	---	62.3	30.3
Interstate payments	---	2800	9.6	50.0	---	13.6	29.2
Foreign currency & precious metals	26000	380	9.6	0.7	---	3.5	3.5
Total	12.5	23.8	39.8	34.7	---	100.0	100.0
Federal budget deficit	17	48	70	180	192		
Net increase of central bank federal debt* &	7	34	40	165	---		
% of its monetization	44	70	57	92	---		
Emission*	27	66	47	89	185		

*   billion of rubles.

Table 19
Prices Dynamics.

	Jan.	Feb.	March	April	May	June	July
Wholesale							
--monthly growth, %	498	175	128	117	123	136	117
--growth in relation to prices until 9/1/91, %	1673	2900	3750	4400	5400	7350	8600
Retail							
--monthly growth, %	350	124	121	114	111	114	107
--growth in relation to prices until 9/1/91, %	878	1089	1318	1500	1670	1900	2030

Source: The National Economy of Russia in January-July 1992. The State Committee on Statistics of Russia.

101

Table 20
Multiplication of Bank Deposits.

	1st quarter	April	May	June	2nd quarter
Monetary basis increase*	147.5	117.9	244.0	297.7	659.6
Money supply increase M1'* Multiplier M1'	241.1 1.63	30.6 0.26	91.8 0.38	270.2 0.91	392.6 0.60
Money supply increase M1 Multiplier M1	413.7 2.80	143.5 1.22	137.9 0.57	478.2 1.61	759.6 1.20
Money supply increase M2* Multipler M2	407.0 2.76	139.4 1.18	130.4 0.54	455.8 1.53	725.6 1.10

* billion rubles

Table 21
The Budget System of Russia. 1991-1992 (% to GNP)

	1992a	1992b
Revenues		
Indirect taxes	15.7	8.9
Income tax	6.3	13.4
Personal taxes	2.0	3.9
Others	5.1	7.5
Total	29.1	33.7
Expenses		
On national economy	12.1	16
Social sphere, R&D	9.1	10
Defense	4.6	7
Government, administrative & legislative bodies	2.0	3
Total	33.3	46
Deficit (-)	-4.2	-12.3
GNP, bln. rbl.	15500	15500

a-ratified by the Supreme Soviet oif Russia
b-authors forecast

Table 22
Main Indices of Privatization Process in Russian Federation in January-August, 1992

	Cumulative During 1 quarter	Results: by 1.06	Results: by 1.08
1. State enterprises with independent balance.	13904	184339	221189
2. Number of privatization applications (compiled).	18366	38843	56167
3. Declined applications.	656	1614	2982
4. Applicationsn being realized.	12677	25560	31851
5. Applications already realized.	5023	4783	12015
6. Pecuniary means gained (mln. rubles).	1893	3817179	01295.19
7. Property value of sold enterprises (mln. rubles).	1171.8	5962.619	19208.08
8. State enterprises reformed into joint-stock companies with shares on sale.	59	85	135
9. Enterprises on lease, including lease with redeem	945116 7581	16017 8413	17924 10464

Data of GKI, RF.

Table 23
Dynamics of "Small" Privatization

	Retail Shops		Cafes, Restaurants		Everyday Services	
	1.07	1.08	1.07	1.08	1.07	1.08
Privatized						
-Total	6523	7600	2100	2300	3871	4800
-% (to the total number)	3.8	4.4	1.5	1.7	3.1	3.8
Reference: the share of enterprises to be privatized by the end of 1992 (%)	60		50		50	

Data of GKI, RF.

Table 24
Industrial and Economic Activity of EFI

	1990	1991	1992 (first six months)	1992 (forecast)
1. Number of working enterprises. The same in the percentage to the number of the registered EFI.	about 700 less than 40	about 1300		1800
2. Number of the employed, thousands of people.		137	about 150	175
3. Wages expenditures mln., rubles.	342	1287		
4. Volume of the implementation of production and services (in the present prices), mln., rubles.	3181	18406	3800* (more than 100000)	300
5. Export (in the external economic prices according to the official exchange rate of the ruble to the hard currency), mln., rubles.	189	422	$656 mln.	$1400 mln.
6. Import (in the external economic prices according to the official exchange rate of the ruble), mln., rubles.	729	470	$358 mln.	$700 mln.
7. Implementation in the hard currency on the Russian market (with the recounting according to the official rate), mln., rubles.	581	986	$188 mln.	$350 mln.
8. Implementation in rubles, mln., rubles.	2458	11278	20000	55000

* The total volume of the implementation of production and services of all joint ventures published by the State Statistical Committee of the RF, 38 billion rubles, ("Economic Newspaper," Issue 30, July 1992) seems to be doubtful. If we use the "average" official exchange rate of the ruble to the US dollar which existed in the first six months (approximately 100 rubles for $1), then the sum of the export of joint ventures in rubles of the sales on the home market in hard currency and in rubles will be more than 100 billion rubles, which seems to be closer to reality. In the same issue, the State Statistic Committee says the increase wholesale prices in industry increased 14.6 times as compared with January-June 1991. Taking into consideration all these facts, even without any growth in production, the volume of the implementation of all joint ventures in January-June 1992 would be 83 billion rubles.